SALMON NATION

PEOPLE, FISH, AND OUR COMMON HOME

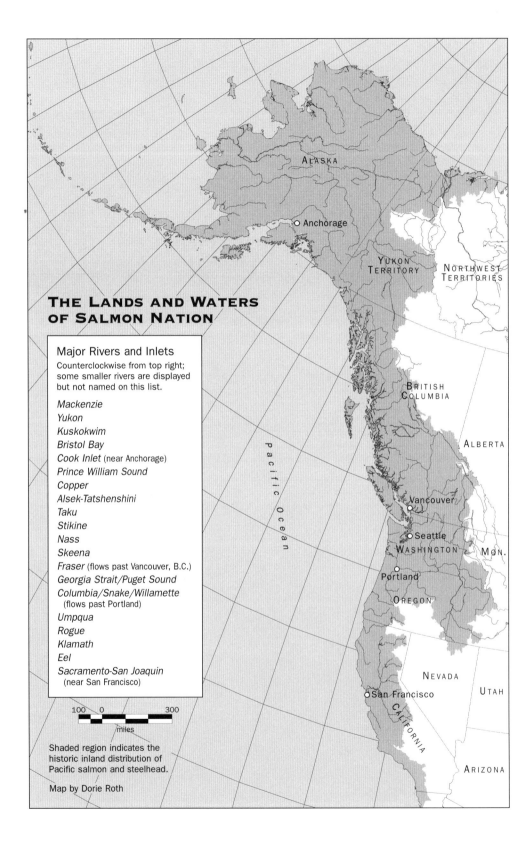

THE LANDS AND WATERS
OF SALMON NATION

Major Rivers and Inlets

Counterclockwise from top right;
some smaller rivers are displayed
but not named on this list.

Mackenzie
Yukon
Kuskokwim
Bristol Bay
Cook Inlet (near Anchorage)
Prince William Sound
Copper
Alsek-Tatshenshini
Taku
Stikine
Nass
Skeena
Fraser (flows past Vancouver, B.C.)
Georgia Strait/Puget Sound
Columbia/Snake/Willamette
  (flows past Portland)
Umpqua
Rogue
Klamath
Eel
Sacramento-San Joaquin
  (near San Francisco)

100   0   300
miles

Shaded region indicates the
historic inland distribution of
Pacific salmon and steelhead.

Map by Dorie Roth

ALASKA

○ Anchorage

YUKON
TERRITORY

NORTHWEST
TERRITORIES

BRITISH
COLUMBIA

ALBERTA

Pacific Ocean

Vancouver
○

○ Seattle
WASHINGTON   MON.

○
Portland

OREGON

NEVADA

UTAH

○ San Francisco

CALIFORNIA

ARIZONA

SALMON NATION

PEOPLE, FISH, AND OUR COMMON HOME

ESSAYS BY

ELIZABETH WOODY

JIM LICHATOWICH

RICHARD MANNING

FREEMAN HOUSE

SETH ZUCKERMAN

AND A PORTFOLIO OF ORIGINAL MAPS BY

DORIE ROTH

EDWARD C. WOLF AND SETH ZUCKERMAN, EDITORS

 ecotrust

PORTLAND, OREGON

Founded in 1991 and based in Portland, Oregon, Ecotrust is a nonprofit organization that works with individuals, organizations, businesses, and government agencies throughout the Pacific Northwest to build Salmon Nation, a place where people and wild salmon thrive.

Ecotrust
721 NW Ninth Ave, Suite 200
Portland, OR 97209
(503) 227-6225
www.ecotrust.org

Library of Congress Control Number: 2003104574
ISBN 0-9676364-1-8

Photo and illustration credits:
p. 8, from the collection of Alex Blendl; p. 9 (inset), Oregon Historical Society (OrHistSo #4463); p. 16, Oregon Historical Society (OHS #682-A, Neg. #OrHi 4697); p. 17 (inset), Oregon Historical Society (OrHis #680, Neg. #OrHi 93325); p. 32, labels from the collection of Matt Winters; p. 33 (inset), Seth Zuckerman; p. 40, Katie Doka; map portfolio: salmon illustrations, Shari Erickson; steelhead illustration, Joe Tomelleri; p. 50, © 1999 Gary Braasch; p. 51 (inset), © 1999 Gary Braasch; pp. 54-55, Steve Blackburn; p. 62, Seth Zuckerman; p. 63 (inset), © Adrian Dorst. Subjects and locations available upon request.

Cover and book design by Bryan Potter Design, Portland, Oregon

Cover illustration by Katie Doka

The text of this book is set in Bookman font.

Detailed information on the data sources consulted in the creation of the maps in this book is available upon written request to Ecotrust.

Elizabeth Woody's essay "Recalling Celilo" is adapted with permission from "TWANAT, to follow behind the ancestors," in *First Fish, First People: Salmon Tales of the North Pacific Rim*, edited by Judith Roche and Meg McHutchinson and published by One Reel and the University of Washington Press, Seattle. © 1998 by One Reel.

Freeman House's essay "Keep the Gift Moving" is excerpted and adapted from *Totem Salmon*, © 1999 by Freeman House, and reprinted by permission of Beacon Press, Boston.

Printed with soy-based inks on recycled paper by Bridgetown Printing Inc. in Portland, Oregon. Text: Casablanca Opaque Smooth Text, 100% recycled fiber, 20% post-consumer; and Endeavor Gloss, 50% recycled fiber, 15% post-consumer, chlorine free. Cover: Tango C1S Cover

Contents

Maps & Illustrations

INTRODUCTION

Along the west coast of North America, people
and salmon have mingled their fates since the end of the last Ice Age.

Several species of Pacific salmon inhabit the waters of this region, from the rain-soaked fjords of Alaska to creeks in the parched country east of the Cascade Mountains.

Human beings have peopled this vast landscape as thoroughly as the salmon have filled its rivers, and we've kept the fish always in our gaze. Every year, with the salmon's age-old migration from ocean to headwaters, people have caught them, eaten them, and celebrated their return. In turn, as people have multiplied and spread across the land, the salmon have come to depend on us to care for the freshwater streams where the fish hatch, grow, and years later, return to spawn.

This shared terrain is Salmon Nation, a territory that spans two countries, six states and one province. Beyond that, it is a state of mind that recognizes this land is not ours alone. We the people of Salmon Nation choose not to turn our backs on these fish.

The salmon reciprocate. Thanks to the nutrients brought inland from the sea by spawning salmon, the trees and earth of this region are built of salmon just as our bones and flesh are partly salmon-made. Native peoples shaped cultures and societies to the rhythms of these migrations and the lessons they offered. Today, we have an opportunity to learn from their example.

To glean this wisdom, we must first understand these fish and our long relationship with them. In the pages of this book, we explore that history. Our story begins with a glimpse of the connection between fish and people during aboriginal times. It explores the sources of recent hardship for salmon and the people who depend on them, and concludes by surveying the prospects for renewing the bond between human and fish. It includes maps that show where the salmon are in trouble, where they've gone extinct, and where they're abundant. You'll discover the difference between wild and farmed salmon fillets, and learn to name the kinds of fishing boats that you see in harbors along our coast.

With words, maps, and images, we invite you home to Salmon Nation, a place where people and fish can thrive together.

FOR AS LONG AS PEOPLE HAVE LIVED ALONG THE NORTH PACIFIC
COAST, THE SALMON HAVE BEEN HERE. ABORIGINAL PEOPLE LIVED
WITH THE FISH FOR CENTURIES, RESPECTFULLY CATCHING WHAT
THEY NEEDED AND TAKING CARE OF THE STREAMS THAT PRODUCED
A HARVEST ESSENTIAL TO THEIR WAY OF LIFE. NATIVE AMERICAN
WRITER ELIZABETH WOODY TAKES US TO CELILO FALLS ON THE
COLUMBIA RIVER, A PLACE WHERE INDIGENOUS RELATIONSHIPS WITH
SALMON PROSPERED FOR AT LEAST TWELVE THOUSAND YEARS;
SHE INTRODUCES US TO WHAT WAS, AND WHAT REMAINS.

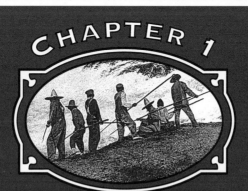

CHAPTER 1

RECALLING CELILO

BY
ELIZABETH WOODY

Along the mid-Columbia River ninety miles

east of Portland, Oregon, stand Celilo Indian Village and Celilo Park.
Beside the eastbound lanes of Interstate 84 are a peaked-roof longhouse
and a large metal building. The houses in the village are older, and easy
to overlook. You can sometimes see nets and boats beside the homes,
though some houses are empty. By comparison, the park is frequently
filled with lively and colorful wind surfers. Submerged beneath the shim-
mering surface of the river lies Celilo Falls, or *Wyam.*

Wyam means "Echo of Falling Water" or "Sound of Water Upon the
Rocks." Located on the fourth-largest North American waterway, it was
one of the most significant fisheries of the Columbia River system. In
recent decades the greatest irreversible change occurred in the middle

Columbia as the Celilo site was inundated by The Dalles Dam on March 10, 1957. The tribal people who gathered there did not believe it possible. The Dalles is one of nineteen dams on the mainstem of the Columbia River built to generate the cheap electric power celebrated by Woody Guthrie in "Roll On, Columbia." Concerns about drowning Celilo carried little weight against the overwhelming public support for the dams and the jobs their construction entailed.

Historically, the *Wyampum* lived at *Wyam* for over twelve thousand years. Estimates vary, but *Wyam* is among the longest continuously inhabited communities in North America. Estimates will always vary, as our tenure in the Western Hemisphere is disputed due to changes in the belief system of the stolid science of archaeology. The elders tell us we have been here from time immemorial.

Today we know Celilo Falls as more than a lost landmark. It was a place as revered as one's own mother. The story of *Wyam*'s life is the story of the salmon, and of my own ancestry. I live with the forty-two-year absence and silence of Celilo Falls, much as an orphan lives hearing of the kindness and greatness of his or her mother.

The original locations of my ancestral villages on the *N'ch-íwana* (Columbia River) are Celilo Village and the *Wishram* village that nestled below the petroglyph, She-Who-Watches or *Tsagaglallal*. My grandmother, Elizabeth Thompson Pitt *(Mohalla)*, was a *Wyampum* descendent and a *Tygh* woman. My grandfather, Lewis Pitt *(Wa Soox Site)*, was a *Wasco*, *Wishram*, and *Watlala* man. But my own connections to Celilo Falls are tenuous at best. I was born two years after Celilo drowned in the backwaters of The Dalles Dam.

My grandfather fished at Celilo with his brother, George Pitt II, at a site that a relative or friend permitted, as is their privilege. They fished on scaffolds above the white water with dip nets. Since fishing locations are inherited, they probably did not have a spot of their own. They were *Wascopum*, not *Wyampum*.

Catching a fish, the fisher hollered "HO!" He would lift the dip net with its wild, powerful fish. My mother and aunt, Charlotte and Lillian, recall riding the dangerous cable cars back and forth over the white water of the falls. This, I imagine, was to my great-uncle's spot. Andrew David *(Tuutawaîsa)* fished on Big Island. My Uncle Lewis, who was preschool age at the time, recalls the hot sands and the indescribable smell of the falls — a smell for which he can find no equivalent today.

When the fish ran, people were wealthy. People from all over the country would come to Celilo to watch the "Indians" catch fish. They would purchase fish freshly caught. It was one of the most famous tourist sites in North America. And many long-time Oregonians and Washingtonians today differentiate themselves from newcomers by their fond memories of Celilo Falls.

What happened at *Wyam* was more significant than entertainment. People gathered here by season through generations across millennia to catch *nusoox* (salmon) and news of relatives from across the river or far away. People celebrated their happiness with horse racing and gambling. Women played card games like *Wa-look-sha* and *Montee* in their free time. People played stick games in the evenings.

During the day, women cleaned large amounts of finely cut fish and hung the parts to dry in the heat of the arid landscape. We ate all of the fish, except for the guts. Nutritionally complete, the fish provided essential nutrients, dried or fresh. Coupled with fruits and roots, the diet was high in calcium, iron, vitamin C, healthy oils, and minerals. Before the upriver dams were built, fishers caught Chinook salmon known as "June hogs." These salmon were unbelievably large, fat and strong for their long journey to distant spawning grounds. I have heard of women who packed these fish four at a time, dragging their tails on the ground behind them. Imagine one seventy-pound fish—and then imagine carrying four of them up a hill! The people at *Wyam* were healthy and strong.

So abundant were the fish passing *Wyam* on their upriver journey that the fish caught there could feed a whole family through the winter. *Chahlīe*, finely pounded dried flesh of the salmon mixed with dried berries, could store for up to two years. The expertly cut dried salmon flesh in drying sheds looked like spread kites. The women dried the heads and gills. Even the spines and tails, with small orange windows of dry flesh between the bones, went eventually into soup. Many families had enough salmon to trade with other tribes or individuals for specialty items. We had Klickitat baskets from such trades. My grandfather's mother, Charlotte Edwards Pitt *(Y-yuten)*, traded her fine pictorial beadwork at *Wyam*, for example.

No one would starve if they could work. Even those incapable of physical work could share other talents. It was a dignified existence. Peaceful, perhaps due in part to the sound of the water that echoed in people's minds and the negative ions produced by the falls. Research has shown this to generate a feeling of well-being in human beings. It is with a certain sense of irony that I note companies now sell machines to generate such ions in the homes of those who can "afford" this feeling of well-being.

Children had a wonderful time at *Wyam*. They would climb the rocks

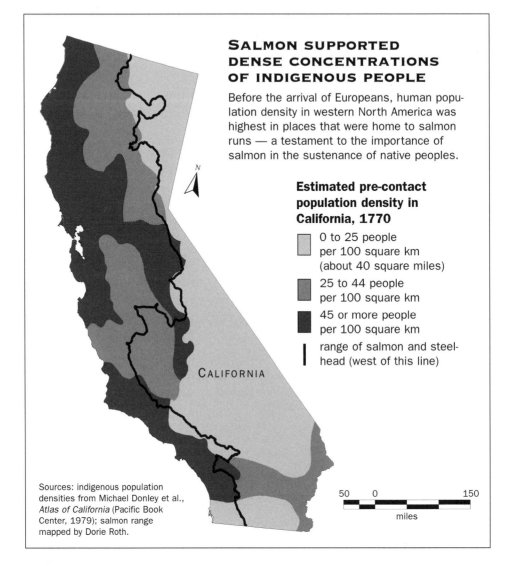

SALMON SUPPORTED DENSE CONCENTRATIONS OF INDIGENOUS PEOPLE

Before the arrival of Europeans, human population density in western North America was highest in places that were home to salmon runs — a testament to the importance of salmon in the sustenance of native peoples.

Estimated pre-contact population density in California, 1770

0 to 25 people per 100 square km (about 40 square miles)

25 to 44 people per 100 square km

45 or more people per 100 square km

range of salmon and steelhead (west of this line)

CALIFORNIA

Sources: indigenous population densities from Michael Donley et al., *Atlas of California* (Pacific Book Center, 1979); salmon range mapped by Dorie Roth.

50   0   150
miles

behind the falls, walking above the chutes that bordered the edge of the river. You became everyone's child when you left your lodging. Relatives and villagers instructed, and occasionally scolded, the children. You had to behave. Every day was school for the young, learning by observation and eventual full participation in the day's activities and work. Young boys began to fish at safer locations in the chutes to learn the skills they would need to move to the more dangerous spots.

It had its risks. The rocks were wet and slippery. One photo from the period shows a boy being fished out of the falls. He had fallen into one of the chutes, and miraculously, he appeared in one of the fishers' dip nets.

Pulled to safety on the platform, he saw another day. Other unwatched children and unlucky fishers were not so fortunate.

An elder woman explained that if my generation knew the language, we would have no questions. We would hear these words directly from the teachings and songs. From time immemorial, the Creator's instruction was direct and clear. Feasts and worship held to honor the first roots and berries are major events. The head and tail of the first salmon caught at Celilo is returned to *N'ch-īwana*. The whole community honored that catch: *One of our relatives has returned, and we consider the lives we take to care for our communities.*

Prayer may no longer be enough to restore the wild runs of salmon. But prayer is neither superficial nor insignificant, as the Columbia River Inter-Tribal Fish Commission has pointed out:

> ". . . great spiritual comfort is derived from the first salmon whose journey ends with a feast held in its honor. Together, tribal members and salmon weave a unique cultural fabric designed by the Divine Creator. What the mind cannot comprehend, the heart and spirit interpret. The result is a beautiful and dignified ceremonial response to the Creator in appreciation for the willingness of Nature to serve humankind."

The songs in the "ceremonial response to the Creator" are repeated seven times by seven drummers, a bell ringer, and people gathered in the Longhouse. *Washat* song is an ancient method of worship. Before the singing, dancers line up from the eldest to the youngest in a circle around the rim of the open floor — a space Chief Thompson called "the open heart of Mother Earth." By wearing the finest Indian dress, the dancers show respect to the Creator. Some have beaded and woven family heirlooms mixed with modern cloth ribbon shirts and bright wing dresses. Those who can do so, stand and rhythmically move their bodies with a bend of their knees. The swinging of cupped hands to hearts signifies the gathering of the songs into their hearts. Some people swing large eagle feathers.

Men on the south side, women on the north, the dancers begin to move. In a pattern of a complete circle they dance sideways, counterclockwise. Some dancers leap high. When they stop, they are north and south again. The drums are in the west, while the east remains open toward the rising sun. The north holds seven stationary drummers and the bell ringer. This ceremony symbolizes the partnership of men and women, the essential equality and balance within the four directions and the cosmos. We each have our place and our role. As a result, the Longhouse is a special place to learn.

Meanwhile, in the kitchen, women prepare the meal. Salmon, venison, edible roots, and the various berries—huckleberries and chokecherries—are the four sacred foods. More common foods are added to these significant four on portable tables. Tule mats on the floor await the people. Long hours have gone into the preparation of the meal. Those who gather the roots and berries are distinguished. Their selection to gather the foods is recognition of good hearts and minds. Tribal men who have hunted and fished are likewise acknowledged. One does not gather food without proper training, so as not to disrupt natural systems.

A prayer is led in song. With instruction in *Sahaptin*, the people take one of each of the sacred four foods to their plates with a cup of water beside. In turn, we take a sample of each and eat a small piece: salmon, venison, roots, and berries. Finally, the water is called for with a loud and long *"Chush!"* We drink and the ritual is complete.

As my uncle explained to his children, "we travel from the river to the mountains with these foods." Even the order in which we taste them travels from *N'ch-īwana* to the white peaks of the volcanic Cascade range. Part of my ancestral geography, these are the mountains now known as Adams and Hood.

What has happened to Celilo Falls illustrates a story of inadequacy and ignorance of this land. The story begins, of course, long before the submergence of the falls with the seed of ambitions to make an Eden where Eden was not needed. One needs to learn from the land how to live upon it.

The mainstem *N'ch-īwana* is today broken up by nineteen hydroelectric dams, many planned and built without a thought for the fish. Nuclear, agricultural, and industrial pollution, the evaporation of water from the reservoirs impounded behind dams, the clearcut mountainsides—all are detrimental to salmon. Since 1855, the *N'ch-īwana*'s fourteen million wild salmon have dwindled to fewer than one hundred thousand.

Traditional awareness counsels in a simple, direct way to take only what we need, and let the rest grow. How can one learn? My uncle reminded me that we learned about simplicity first. He said, "The stories your grandmother told. Remember when she said her great grandmother, *Kah-Nee-Ta*, would tell her to go to the river and catch some fish for the day? Your grandmother would catch several fish, because she loved to look at them. She would let all but two go. Her grandmother taught her that."

A larger sorrow shadows my maternal grandmother's story of the childhood loss of the material and intangible. What if the wild salmon no longer return? I cannot say whether we have the strength necessary to bear this impending loss.

The salmon, the tree, and even Celilo Falls *(Wyam)* echo within if we become still and listen. Once you have heard, take only what you need and let the rest go.

WITH THE ARRIVAL OF EUROPEANS IN THE WEST, THE RELATIONSHIP OF PEOPLE AND SALMON CHANGED DRAMATICALLY. THE NEW SETTLERS' VALUES DIFFERED GREATLY FROM THOSE OF THE ABORIGINAL INHABITANTS, AND THEIR CHOICES MADE THE STREAMS OF SALMON NATION LESS HOSPITABLE TO FISH. TODAY, THE CLAMOR THAT SALMON ONCE CAUSED WHEN THEY RETURNED TO SPAWN HAS BEEN MUTED AND IN SOME PLACES EVEN STILLED. THIS CHAPTER EXPLORES WHY.

CHAPTER 2

MUDDIED WATERS, MUDDLED THINKING
BY JIM LICHATOWICH & SETH ZUCKERMAN

The huge trees and untamed landscapes of

the Pacific Northwest impress newcomers and long-time residents alike as miraculous gifts of nature. Not the least among the region's gifts are its salmon runs: Consider that close to a million wild and hatchery-bred salmon each year make their journeys up the Columbia River to spawn, and the number sounds impressive.

Today's fish runs pale, however, compared with the abundance that greeted the first white settlers in the nineteenth century. Not one million, but ten to sixteen million salmon used to run up the Columbia annually. And that is just a small part of the tale of decline that salmon fisheries have sustained in California, Oregon, Washington, and parts of British Columbia for more than one hundred years.

The problem first attracted attention when the region's production of canned fish began to drop early in this century. Now it has worsened to affect not only commercial and sport fishing, but also the very survival of many runs of fish. From the redwood-covered hills of coastal California through the waterways of metropolitan Portland and Seattle to the arid country east of the Cascades, salmon populations have been listed as "endangered" or "threatened" under the Endangered Species Act. For some runs, however, this level of concern has come too late. At least 232 genetically unique groups of Pacific salmon and steelhead are known to have disappeared entirely, losses that have occurred across a startlingly large portion of the salmon's natural range.

Discussions of the causes of this decline often seem like a sort of lunatic firing squad in which people form a circle and shoot at whoever's across from them. City folks blame the dams, and upriver farmers with irrigated fields blame commercial fishermen. The fishermen blame recreational anglers and loggers, loggers blame climate change and cattle in the creeks, and cattle ranchers blame predatory sea lions and merganser ducks. Everyone blames the deep-ocean trawlers and drift-net fisheries for scooping up immature salmon and the sea-life on which they feed. Each of these actions has hurt the salmon, but they are all manifestations of a more profound failing that has driven the Pacific salmon into a tailspin.

Like people everywhere, the Euro-American settlers who began to arrive in the Pacific Northwest two lifetimes ago displayed the whole range of human nature. Some proved capable of wanton damage to their new home, while others were concerned by the toll their presence seemed to take. The impacts of the worst were amplified, and the moderating influence of the best was muted, because so few glimpsed the connections among the parts of the system — fish, trees, rivers. Even those who did could scarcely envision the losses in store, as the trickle of early settlers turned to a flood swelled by the power of industrial development.

In the nineteenth century, human use of the land and its resources in the near term seemed more important than protecting ecological bounty in perpetuity. Surrounded by native abundance, those settlers acted as though the riches of nature were put there expressly for people — an attitude that recurs throughout the history of the West.

Even when the early white settlers and their descendants took steps to improve conditions for the salmon, the effects often fell short of what was intended. Quick to assume that we understood how nature worked, we have sometimes hurt what we were trying to protect. Salmon have

NATURAL HISTORY OF THE PACIFIC SALMON

Although the six species of Pacific salmon (like their distant relatives the Atlantic salmon) spend most of their lives at sea, they spawn in freshwater, homing in on the rivers of their birth. They swim upstream, often traversing hundreds of miles en route to small waterways where their size as full-grown returning adults makes them seem out of proportion to their surroundings. The female uses her body to dig a depression in the gravel, where she lays her eggs while a male hovers at her side to fertilize them. She then moves upstream and flaps her tail against the stream bottom, covering the eggs with a protective layer of gravel. The eggs incubate in this nest, known as a "redd," where they depend on the flow of water through the spaces between the rocks to carry vital oxygen to the developing embryos.

After a couple of months, the fry swim up through the gravel and begin to feed on small aquatic insects. Salmon are most at home in water colder than 60 degrees F. Depending on the species and race of fish, temperatures of 65 to 70 degrees can be stressful or even lethal at this age. After a period ranging from a few days (in the case of pink and chum salmon) to as much as a year and a half (in the case of steelhead or coho), the fingerlings swim downstream to the ocean, where they spend between one and five years migrating and feeding across thousands of miles of open water before returning to their home rivers to spawn. The salmon's ability to find their natal streams was a mystery for many years. Although their ability to navigate to the mouths of the rivers is still not perfectly understood, we know that their sense of smell guides them once they enter fresh water.

Because salmon return to their native streams to reproduce, they divide naturally into distinct populations that rarely interbreed with their neighbors. Each population, or "stock," adapts to the conditions of its home river.

The salmon's sense of direction is not perfect, however, and some fish do stray from one river system to the next — which enables surrounding healthy populations to recolonize streams where the salmon runs have been extinguished. This straying tends to take place within certain bounds. Straying behavior, plus other factors including life history, geography, the geology of home streams, and genetics, is involved in the designation of "evolutionarily significant units" by regulators applying the Endangered Species Act. For instance, the coastal rivers from the mouth of the Columbia River south to Santa Cruz, California, are divided into four such units and the rivers of the Columbia Basin into five.

been raised in hatcheries and released into streams where, as we will see later, they have done more harm than good. Well-intentioned people restoring salmon habitat in the 1970s dismantled logjams and dragged wood out of streams, only to find twenty years later that the creeks need some of that wood back in the channel.

Despite the best intentions, our actions on behalf of fish have time and again reflected a readiness to tinker with an ecosystem we did not fully understand, and a failure to comprehend the results. No amount of hard work or money can overcome the shortcomings of an approach to salmon management built on such shaky foundations. If we are to coexist with wild salmon, it is up to this generation to figure out how.

The first unprecedented impact on salmon, less economic than political, emerged during the fur trade era in the 1830s. Trappers in the employ of Britain's Hudson's Bay Company attempted to trap beavers to extinction as far south as Oregon's Willamette Valley. Seeking to deny the fledgling United States an economic base in a region the Americans intended to possess as part of their Manifest Destiny, the trappers inadvertently hurt the region's fish in the process. Beaver dams, once ubiquitous throughout the Pacific Northwest, provide critical nursery habitat for young fish, particularly in the dry intermountain region.

The salmon's troubles escalated when white settlers from the East Coast introduced a new technology for preserving fish. The first cannery was established on a raft in California's Sacramento River in 1864. Two years later, the canners moved north in search of a steadier supply of fish, which cannery operators found on the Columbia River. By canning the fish, these early entrepreneurs gained access to markets for virtually unlimited quantities of salmon in the eastern United States and Europe. Fishing was not managed to ensure the perpetuation of the species. In their rush to catch as many fish as possible, commercial fishermen often delivered far more salmon than canneries could process, and workers simply shoveled the excess back into the rivers. It wasn't long before the catch in the Columbia and other rivers peaked and began its long decline, interrupted only by particularly fecund years.

In the eastern and southern parts of the salmon's range, irrigation played a large role in the salmon's decline. Streams in the dry interior valleys such as the Yakima and the Sacramento once harbored huge populations of salmon, which thrived in the region's snow-fed rivers. With the advent of irrigated agriculture, the fish suffered a series of insults. Many fingerlings strayed into gravity-fed ditch systems on their way downstream where their lives ended in a furrow; countless others were sucked out of the streams by irrigation pumps introduced since the nineteen thirties. In the delta of the Sacramento and San Joaquin rivers, the power of pumps sending water south is so great that it changes the direction of flow, tricking fish into migrating toward the pumping stations instead of toward the ocean. In Oregon, the National Research Council estimates that fewer than one thousand of the fifty-five thousand stream diversions are properly screened to keep fish from being diverted along with the water.

As farmers shunt more water to their fields, less remains in the stream. Natural pools become shallower and in some cases dry up entirely. The less water, the less protection the fish have from predators, and the quicker the water warms. Yet the infrastructure for irrigation was put in place before anyone considered the effects of water diversion. As we come to understand its implications, we realize that people have built their lives and expectations around the use of that water, making it difficult to accommodate the fish.

Livestock grazing has also had a serious impact on fish. In much of the arid West, cattle prefer to spend their time along streambanks, where they eat the young willows and cottonwoods that would otherwise shade the stream and contribute to its stability. Even their foot-traffic, up and down the banks, tends to increase erosion. Rendered bare and silty, streams are less hospitable to salmon. This was rarely the ranchers' intention; few considered the possibility that cattle would harm fish. Initially, at least, it would have been seen simply as part of the price of settling the West.

By the latter decades of the nineteenth century, commercial loggers moved into the coastal valleys. They logged the riverbanks first, rarely ranging more than a mile away from the water — about as far as oxen could economically haul giant old-growth logs. Lacking the technology to easily build roads to haul timber to the mill, early loggers used "splash dams" instead. They would dam the stream with a temporary wooden structure, then drag the logs into the pool that built up behind the dam. Later, the dam was blown with explosives, flushing water and logs downstream in a wall of debris. These man-made torrents scoured the channel clean of the vegetation and naturally fallen logs that provided habitat for the juvenile fish and their insect prey. They also gouged the stream bottom down to bedrock, removing the gravel needed by salmon to spawn. Coastal streams in California, Oregon, and Washington are still recovering from the effects of this practice, many decades after it ceased.

As logging technologies modernized, their effects spread further from the waterways. The invention of the bulldozer and the gasoline-powered chainsaw, coupled with the building boom that followed World War II, spread logging across the landscape, leaving a web of roads behind.

Roads tend to concentrate run-off from its many natural pathways into muddy roadside ditches, which eventually dump their dirty water into streams. Poorly designed roads wash out easily, sending even more sediment into creeks. Although road-building practices have improved somewhat, hundreds of thousands of miles of logging roads, some of them abandoned, continue to threaten salmon habitat. (Roads used for residential access, recreation, mining or ranching can be equally destructive if not well built and maintained.)

Aggressive logging itself can cause erosion. Trees shield the ground from the harsh impact of rainstorms, and their roots bind the soil together. A few landslides below clear-cut logging (where all the trees are removed from a site) have gained notoriety when they killed downslope residents or demolished their houses, but hundreds more take place in the backcountry without attracting much human attention. Salmon notice them all.

Whether from road-building, other human causes, or natural landslides, erosion deposits sediment in the streams. Sand and silt cloud the water and can damage the gills of fish, while the larger particles — from gravel on up — fill in the pools that provide good habitat for fish. Some of the worst erosion occurred when miners washed whole hillsides through their sluiceboxes in pursuit of gold during the nineteenth century. The rivers of the Sierra Nevada and the Klamath-Siskiyou (among others) still bear the effects of that era.

Dams present another set of problems — obstacles to fish passage up or down the river. High dams such as Grand Coulee on the Columbia River and Shasta on the Sacramento were built without provision for the salmon to get around them, choking off thousands of miles of spawning habitat upriver on the Snake, the upper Columbia, and rivers of the Sierra Nevada. Even where access was provided with fish ladders (a series of stair-stepped pools), the tamed rivers often became inhospitable to the juvenile salmon headed downstream. Long slack-water lakes lack the current that cues the fingerlings about which direction to travel, and the floods of spring snow-melt, bottled up behind the dams, no longer speed the young fish to the sea. Some fish are killed by their passage through hydroelectric turbines. Others suffer a bends-like syndrome when spilled over the top of high dams to the churning waters downstream. These dam-related problems are so severe that federal agencies on the Columbia River have taken to transporting fingerlings downstream by barge—perhaps the ultimate human attempt to substitute for the natural functioning of the salmon system.

As urban centers have grown and the suburbs sprawled beyond them, the threats they pose to fish have become more significant. Rain carries the taints of used motor oil, tire rubber, and other effluents of industrial life from city streets into the waterways. Homes, offices, and factories are constructed right up to the edge of streams, clearing the shade that keeps the water cool in summer, and stripping away the plants that contribute to a creek's food chain. Invasive ornamentals such as English ivy displace native plants that contribute to the salmon's habitat and nourish its prey. Flood-control agencies straighten streams and developers fill wetlands, destroying important fish nurseries. Thirsty cities draw on surrounding rivers for their water supply, reducing the flow in local streams. Ironically, this dependence is a two-sided coin. Erosion that threatens to muddy the water for fish also clouds municipal water supplies and fills reservoirs with sediment. So the cities' reliance on rivers can create a powerful political constituency to protect urban water supplies, thereby protecting salmon habitat.

All of these factors make a point about salmon that is hard, even today, for many people to appreciate fully: though waterborne, salmon don't just live in streams, they live in watersheds. Everything that happens to flowing water, from ridgetop to rivulet to river itself, affects the health of salmon. For decades, many of these connections were unknown; land managers treated elements of the forest-and-fish system as isolated parts. Now we know better, but we battle the inertia of more than a century of treating the Pacific Northwest as a warehouse of provisions instead of a living system of which we are but one member.

When commercial fishing for salmon began on the West Coast in the 1860s, fishermen took advantage of a natural abundance that had sustained the indigenous people for thousands of years. Astonished early observers described enormous quantities of salmon that spooked horses

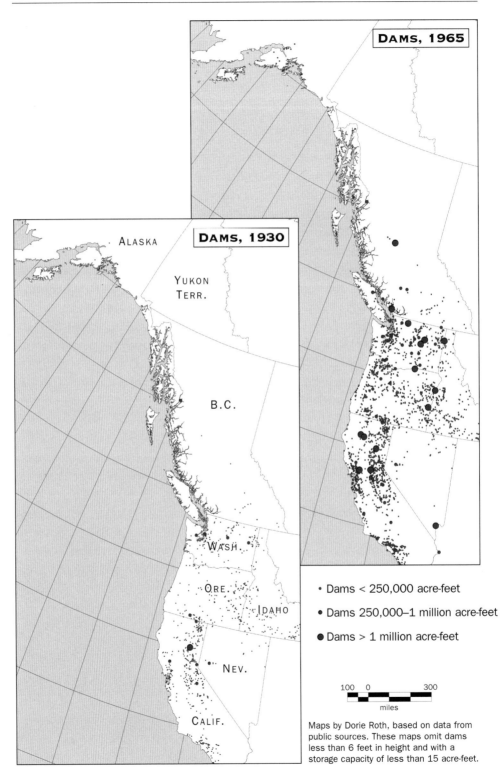

DAMS, 1965

DAMS, 1930

ALASKA

YUKON
TERR.

B.C.

WASH.

ORE.

IDAHO

NEV.

CALIF.

· Dams < 250,000 acre-feet

• Dams 250,000–1 million acre-feet

● Dams > 1 million acre-feet

100   0   300
miles

Maps by Dorie Roth, based on data from
public sources. These maps omit dams
less than 6 feet in height and with a
storage capacity of less than 15 acre-feet.

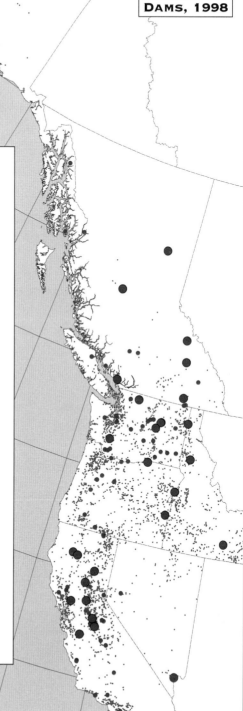

DAMS, 1998

DAMS HAVE CAUSED WIDESPREAD DAMAGE TO SALMON HABITAT

The spread of dams in the southern part of the region has posed a major threat to the salmon, in some cases completely barring the upstream migration of the fish. Runs have dwindled even above dams equipped with fish ladders — stair-stepped cascades of artificial pools. In the reservoirs that dams create, no current guides juvenile salmon to the ocean. Dams catch the peak run-off for use later in the year, eliminating the spring freshets that speed fish to the sea, and restraining high winter flows that otherwise fill the river and enable adults of winter runs to reach their spawning grounds.

- • Dams whose normal capacity is less than 250,000 acre-feet
- ● Dams whose normal capacity is between 250,000 and 1 million acre-feet
- ⬤ Dams whose normal capacity is more than 1 million acre-feet

  (An acre-foot is enough water to cover one acre to the depth of one foot.)

100   0   300
miles

as fish splashed their way up creeks, and whitened stream banks with their spawned-out carcasses.

Less than a decade after the first canneries opened, business and political leaders wondered whether this industry could sustain itself. They petitioned Spencer Baird, the first head of the newly formed U.S. Fish Commission, for his advice about how to maintain salmon supplies. With what may strike us as remarkable foresight, Baird warned in 1875 that habitat alteration, dam construction, and overfishing would eventually destroy the Pacific salmon industry.

Despite the future he foresaw, Baird believed that it could not be averted by restrictive regulations. He'd seen such rules fail to save the Atlantic salmon on the other side of the continent. His advice? An investment of $15,000 to $20,000 in artificial propagation to make salmon so abundant that no regulation would be needed. Baird made this recommendation just three years after the first Pacific salmon hatchery had opened on the Sacramento River, before its first complete brood of juvenile chinook salmon had even returned to spawn.

Within decades, salmon hatcheries had become central to decisions made about many West Coast rivers. Their popularity was not based on scientific evidence, because such evidence had neither been sought nor found. Instead, hatcheries were popular because they fit with prevailing social and economic values. In the second half of the 19th century, unfettered access to the resources of the American West was endorsed, encouraged, and subsidized by the government. Hatcheries justified this unregulated access.

The new states of the Pacific Northwest embraced hatcheries and established bureaucracies to build and manage them. The assumptions they embodied amounted to a dogma: that nature is wasteful and profligate, that humans know better, that we should manage nature for the benefit of our own species, and that we can tinker with it as one might adjust an engine or a wind-up clock. By 1910, 500 million artificially propagated salmon were being planted in Pacific coastal streams each year. Fisheries managers counted on hatcheries to maintain future supplies; the fate of the canning industry rested on artificial propagation. But still managers did not evaluate the hatcheries' success, preferring what one writer called in 1930 an "almost idolatrous faith" in this technological fix.

This faith stemmed not from an absence of science, but from a predisposition rooted in the worldview of the time, which held that scientific knowledge granted humans control over nature. Left to her own

FISH RUNS THROUGHOUT THE REGION ARE INFLUENCED BY HATCHERIES

For several decades, hatcheries were seen — incorrectly — as substitutes for healthy rivers, and were used to rationalize projects such as dams that degrade salmon habitat. Hatcheries had already become pervasive in the Northwest by the time it became clear that they were contributing to the salmon's decline. Hatchery salmon diminish the genetic diversity of wild stocks by interbreeding with them, and they compete with wild fish on their way to the ocean.

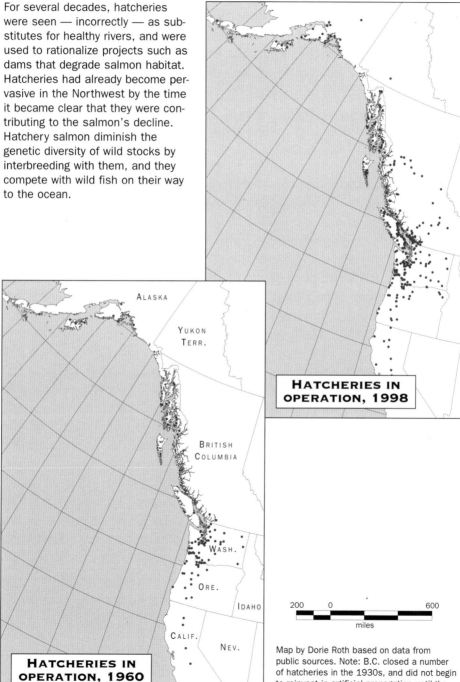

HATCHERIES IN OPERATION, 1998

HATCHERIES IN OPERATION, 1960

200   0   600

miles

Map by Dorie Roth based on data from public sources. Note: B.C. closed a number of hatcheries in the 1930s, and did not begin to reinvest in artificial propagation until the 1960s.

devices, nature was inefficient and wasteful; it was human responsibility to control the natural world, make it more efficient, and harness parts of it, like salmon, fully to human use. Here's how Livingston Stone, an early and enthusiastic advocate of fish culture, explained in 1884 the surplus of wild salmon eggs laid each year in the gravels of the Columbia River: "Nature . . . produces great quantities of seed that nature does not utilize or need. It looks like a vast store that has been provided for nature, to hold in reserve against the time when the increased population of the earth should need it and the sagacity of man should utilize it."

By 1910, "conservation" had joined the political lexicon, but with a rather different meaning than it has today. Conservationists of the early twentieth century devoted little effort to curtailing development or resource exploitation. Instead, they focused on using newfound scientific knowledge to control and thereby improve natural systems through technical expertise and bureaucratic organization.

Hatcheries fit this attitude, as part of a plan to make full use of a watershed or river basin. Up and down the river, crops could be irrigated, cattle grazed, trees cut, power generated. Thanks to artificial propagation, all of this could be done without diminishing the fishery. Hatchery-raised fish no longer needed an ecosystem or watershed, according to this thinking—all they needed was a simple conduit to the sea.

About the same time that questions about the efficacy of hatcheries began to emerge in the 1930s and 1940s, fisheries biologists faced the prospect of massive irrigation and hydroelectric power development in the major salmon rivers of the Pacific Northwest. By that time, biologists understood what the dams would do to fish runs, particularly on the Columbia River. But the social momentum behind the dams and the promise of electric power was unstoppable. State and federal fish agencies once more chose to maintain the status quo — nearly complete dependence on hatcheries to offset lost natural production of fish.

In time, these juvenile salmon factories came to be seen as a public utility just like the electric power grid and the shipping locks, each producing goods and services for public consumption. Nearly forty years would pass before the biologists' fundamental doubts about hatcheries resurfaced. In the meantime, fish produced in captivity were beginning to weaken wild stocks.

It might seem counter-intuitive that hatcheries could actually harm the species being propagated. After all, if the problem is too few fish, why not simply hatch some more? The reason lies in the subtle connections between elements of the salmon system.

The earliest hatcheries were simply egg-incubating stations that released tiny fry into the streams, hoping to increase fish populations by reducing the mortality of eggs incubated in stream-bottom gravels. By the second decade of the twentieth century, managers began to feed the fry and raise them to fingerling size before turning them loose. But the diet they received — a mixture of fish offal, horse meat, tripe, and condemned pork and beef — was ineffective, and even spread disease through the tightly packed schools of fish.

It wasn't until 1960, with the advent of pelletized feed made from fishmeal, that hatcheries had significant success in raising large numbers of fish to large fingerling size or even to the smolting stage, when the fish begin to adapt to salt water for their adult lives.

Even as they became more proficient at raising juvenile fish, the hatcheries were actually undermining the vitality of the wild stocks of salmon that they hoped to supplement. One problem was rooted in "carrying capacity," the maximum number of fish that a particular stream can support. As hatcheries infused rivers with millions of fingerlings for their journeys to the sea, the hatchery fry came to compete with the wild fish traveling oceanward at the same time. At times, there simply wasn't enough food to nourish all of the young fish, to the detriment of both wild and hatchery stocks.

When hatchery-bred fish return as adults and interbreed with wild salmon, they produce offspring that are less hardy than their purely wild counterparts. Each river and tributary has a distinct strain of fish, the product of generations of natural selection in which the fish that best fit a particular environment were the most likely to return and reproduce, passing on their genes to the next generation. For instance, fish whose spawning journey takes them just a few miles from the ocean enter the river nearly ready to mate, while their cousins destined for spawning grounds far inland will not be ready to lay their eggs until months after they re-enter fresh water. In addition, wild fish often possess resistance to the parasites and diseases of their native streams.

Sometimes the genetic wires get crossed accidentally, as when hatchery fish stray into another stream upon returning to spawn. In many other cases, managers transplanted fingerlings from one river system to another. Either way, the hatchery-bred salmon mated with wild native fish and diluted their local adaptations. For example, native coho salmon possess resistance to a particular parasite that is present in coastal Oregon's Nehalem River. Young hatchery coho from another river, where the parasite isn't prevalent, were planted in a tributary of the Nehalem for several years. Later, when adults were collected there, their offspring proved less resistant to the parasite than the wild stocks but not as susceptible as the hatchery transplants. Researchers concluded that the mixing of the stocks had reduced the population's resistance to the parasite. In another case, scientists found that eggs laid by coho of hatchery descent that spawned in the wild were less likely to survive than the eggs of wild fish. The reason? Apparently, the hatchery fish were spawning earlier in the year, which was not as well matched to the conditions of that river as the native salmon's timing.

Finally, even if the hatchery program yields many adults, if those adult fish are targeted by a commercial fishery that captures fish from a combination of stocks — in the ocean where fish from many rivers mingle together, or in the lower reaches of a large river system like the Columbia, for example — the weaker wild stocks will be overharvested. Regulators will devise rules that will allow, say, two-thirds of the stronger stocks to be taken. But those rules will result in a two-thirds harvest of the weaker stocks, whose population will be harmed by such a large loss. Currently, some 80 percent of the adult spawners returning to the Columbia River are the product of hatcheries. Regulations that serve the majority of salmon are unlikely to match the needs of the wild 20 percent.

An indiscriminate hatchery program treats fish like interchangeable parts in a large machine. The first precaution of intelligent tinkering, counseled conservationist Aldo Leopold, is to save all the parts. Neglecting this precaution, we have unbalanced an intricate system and placed the salmon in danger.

Through the lens of history, we can understand our predecessors' decisions that led to the salmon's current straits. But for the last decade or two, we have known better, and some salmon advocates are trying to craft a new approach that runs counter to the assumptions that led to the decisions and choices of the past. The new approach seeks to:

- Restore and protect natural ecological processes, rather than circumventing them with artificial substitutes.
- Control human behaviors that destroy ecological processes, rather than trying to control nature.
- Promote biological and habitat diversity, rather than seeking to improve the production process by simplifying it.

For the first time in a century, many northwesterners openly question whether we ought to exert complete control over the region's rivers. The possibility of removing or breaching mainstem dams on the Columbia and Snake Rivers to restore the fish is now debated in public, a debate that would have been unthinkable as recently as five years ago.

However, it is time-consuming and difficult to change deeply held values and assumptions. Often they become enshrined in laws and institutions that perpetuate old thinking. They bolster accumulations of economic power, which spill over into the political arena and make it difficult to adopt policies that will change our relation to rivers and the landscape. We can still only speculate whether we have the ability to move quickly enough to save Pacific salmon over a significant portion of their natural range.

No one set out to destroy these fish. As a group, salmon regulators, hatchery managers, and fish biologists are hard-working professionals dedicated to maintaining the "supply" of salmon. But their intentions went awry because of the beliefs behind their actions. No amount of good intentions and hard work can overcome the limitations of programs based on faulty assumptions.

Why has it proved impossible to protect the salmon resource, to prevent a century of decline and extinction even though the causes of decline were known and acknowledged from the outset? Politicians, scientists, and most citizens believed in reshaping and managing the landscape to meet our short-term needs. We believed we had the wisdom and ability to simplify and control ecosystems, to make them more productive. We held these beliefs deeply enough to overlook signs of failure even as they clamored for our attention.

Can we think differently about nature in time to make a difference?

SALMON

FIDALGO ISLAND CANNING CO. KETCHICAN, ALASKA

SEA-BIRD BRAND

NET WT.
15½ OZ.

VACUUM PACKED
BY
POINT ADAMS PACKING CO.
HAMMOND — OREGON.

COLUMBIA RIVER
SALMON

PACKED WITH
SALMON OIL
AND SALT

ED WITH
MON OIL
D SALT

PILLAR
ROCK
BRAND

ROYAL CHINOOK
ALMON

COLUMBIA

NET CONTENTS 7¾ OZ.

PACKED BY
PILLAR ROCK
PACKING CO.
PILLAR ROCK,
WAHKIAKUM CO.
WASH.

SPRING PACK

RIVER

PILLAR ROCK
BRAND
ROYAL CHINOOK

SALMON

FRESH

CONTENTS
OON..AS OPENED

SALMON
PACKED BY THE FIDALGO ISLAND PACKING CO.
ANACORTES, WASH.

RED STAR

BRAND

TRADE

CONTENTS 7½ OZ.
PACKED BY
SEUFERT BROS.
PACKING CO.
THE DALLES, ORE.

TENINO BRAND

SALMO COLUMBIA RIVER GAIRDNERI
SALMON

NET WEIGHT 15½ OZ.

NET WEIGHT 15½ OZ.
FINEST QUALITY
SPRING CATCH

VACUUM PACKED
BY
POINT ADAMS PACKING CO.
HAMMOND,
OREGON.

UNTIL THE 1970S, NUMEROUS TOWNS, CULTURES AND WAYS
OF LIFE REVOLVED AROUND PACIFIC SALMON. A FEW STILL DO.
ENVIRONMENTAL WRITER RICHARD MANNING GUIDES US TO A PLACE
WHERE THE HUMAN ECONOMY WAS ONCE TIED TO LOCAL SALMON
RUNS, AND CHARTS THE SHIFTING ECONOMIC TIDES — AND CHANGES IN
THE NATURE OF COMMERCIAL FISHING ITSELF — THAT HAVE STRANDED
FISHING TOWNS FROM CALIFORNIA TO BRITISH COLUMBIA.

CHAPTER 3

GHOST TOWN

BY
RICHARD MANNING

Bad policy prints out in ghost towns. Namu,

British Columbia, is one such town, a proper place for considering the
consequences of economic decisions. Namu is especially appropriate for
our consideration, because it is especially haunting. It looks as if it was
abandoned just a few months ago: its post office, café, and pub on piers
still appear ready for business, its machine shop still workable, its rows
and racks of machinery only rusted some. Namu was a cannery town,
one of more than eighty such sites now strung the length of the coast of
British Columbia north of Vancouver Island, once vital, now all abandoned. Once its residents packed salmon. Now the salmonberry tangles
and sprouting cedar lap at its edges, ready to suck it beneath the waves
of forest.

Namu haunts especially because of the houses, rows of them stretched up the hills, the school and the gutted gym, the segregated housing of Chinese, Japanese, and native cannery workers: segregated, but houses nonetheless, all now empty. Homes, more than machine shops, give evidence that people made lives here, livelihoods now gone.

Ghost towns are no anomaly in North America's cut-and-run resource west. We explain their existence by saying that progress entails change. A mine plays out, a mill closes, a fish run goes to ruin and we move on. Namu, however, harbors a more unsettling set of specters than our mythology has prepared us to confront.

At the mouth of the Namu River, just below the now-crumbling row of shacks that housed native families, a line of rocks reveals itself with each day's ebb tides. These rocks are famous among archaeologists, the remnants of a fish trap six thousand years old. Just above the river's mouth, only fifty feet or so up a bank on a bit of hill, there lies a pit that yielded a worked block of stone, artifice half again as ancient as the fish trap. The stone was most likely a sinker, a fisherman's sinker, at nine thousand years old one of the oldest pieces of tackle on our continent. People — aboriginal, European, and Asian — have made a living fishing at Namu for at least nine thousand years, from the day some fishermen dropped that stone sinker until the late nineteen-eighties when Namu's corporate owners, Weston Foods, closed the cannery and hence the town. Community here spanned the chasm of European colonialism. Something else unsettled it much later.

It would be easy to take the customary exit from this argument, to cite not people but numbers of people, and suggest that the crush of human population worldwide fished out Namu and in the name of efficiency had to move on. Not so fast. To begin with, there are still salmon at Namu, but a different sort of system hauls them away. A system that doesn't need people constituted in small communities.

More importantly, however, the archaeologists tell us that coastal British Columbia and Alaska, the foothold of human population in North America, likely supported one of the densest populations of native peoples in this hemisphere, certainly the densest in what is now Canada. This coast did so almost solely on salmon and cedar. Further, these people annually harvested, for periods of thousands of years, as much salmon as are caught today from the same areas. Most of the world's wild-caught salmon still comes from these areas. In our time it is the fashion to endlessly debate definitions of sustainability, yet the history of the Pacific's northern coast until only just recently stands as a definition for anyone to read.

This argument is not about Namu. Rather, it is about efficiency, about making a living, and about what we mean by progress. We worry that all of the fish will be gone, but the lesson of Namu is that the people are gone, and it is worth examining the connection.

One could not design a better creature on which to base culture than the salmon. It does an enormous amount of work. It hatches from pea-sized eggs in rain-forest streams, migrates to the oceans when it weighs about an ounce, ranges thousands of miles over the course of three to six years, then returns precisely to its native stream weighing ten, fifteen, thirty, even sixty pounds. In terms of raw biological economics, the salmon focuses enormous energy with pinpoint accuracy on a given place. We can think of this, as native peoples did, in terms of food, but First Nations fishers took only a small portion of the fish that migrated annually to streams. Most spawned, died, and rotted, feeding new rounds of fish, animals, and trees. Up to sixty percent of the nutrients of young fish and seventeen percent of the nutrients in streamside rain forest vegetation comes from spawned-out salmon. The basin of the Columbia River alone was once fertilized by the return of nearly two hundred million pounds of fish each year in salmon runs now gone.

The service here is importation: a given community of salmon concentrates this energy, this mass derived from a wide range of sea to a single, predictable point, a place, a Namu. This motion is the engine that drives an entire ecosystem, the power to pull community.

It is as if a rancher in Alberta could release his calves at two hundred pounds each, to range unattended and free (in the economic sense, too) for a few years as far south as Texas and Oklahoma. Imagine that some would return to the rancher's front gate on a given and predictable day. True, not all would return, but those that did, had they undergone the same proportional weight gain as a salmon, would each weigh about fifty thousand pounds. An Alberta rancher would suggest this is a formula for wealth and leisure, and the record of native art along the coast from Northern California to Alaska would suggest the same.

Accounting for the squandering of this wealth begins with the fact that fish traps, the predominant system of harvest for First Nations people and for whites in the early days of the commercial canneries a century ago, are now all relics. The gill net boats, the one- and two-man putt-putts that worked the river mouths and sloughs ever since, are fast becoming antiques as well. They in turn are being replaced by multi-million-dollar aluminum seine net boats that range the offshore waters, and trollers that catch the salmon far at sea. To climb aboard one of these boats is to understand the tenacity of predation. Scramble over a tangle of nets and floats, oil jugs and tools into a cluttered cabin to see sonar, computer monitors, satellite-based guidance systems, and digitized maps recording fish runs and ocean-floor topography.

All this technology catches no more fish than a six-thousand-year-old fish trap once caught. Satellites are not needed to catch salmon, not even to catch a declining number of salmon. The fish would still come back to community, if we would wait. Technology is needed not to beat the fish, but to beat other fishermen. In this race from riverfront fish trap to gill-net boat to troller, each move takes us ever further to sea. One is reminded of the old joke about two men entering grizzly bear country. One of them stops to put on a pair of extra-fast running shoes. The other laughs and says, "You can't outrun a bear," to which his companion replies, "I don't have to. I just have to outrun you."

Fishing boats are sleek machines that seem elegant only in isolation — just one of the many types of machines that run the modern salmon system. Hatcheries are another, in a network of more than three hundred such facilities stretching from California to Alaska, mostly clustered in the south of that region.

The hatchery program predates large dams, and even predates the overfishing that occurred as canneries began exporting the region's biomass to feed the industrial workers of England. Hatcheries spread as salmon runs were over-harvested and depleted, and spread further as habitat was lost to logging, dams, and development in general. We have traditionally blamed catastrophic declines in salmon numbers on the latter causes and viewed hatcheries as a solution. The beneficence of hatcheries was an article of faith, untested until only very recently. Now evidence has mounted that the opposite is true, that streams with hatcheries, when compared to those without, showed a decrease in overall production of fish. Ill-conceived solutions become problems.

Evolution has finely tuned native salmon to the conditions of each particular river, each particular community, and a glut of imported hatchery fish without benefit of this sophisticated tuning greatly skews the picture. So does the release of millions of hungry young mouths without regard for natural food cycles. Simple machines go awry in complex situations.

The question "How awry?" is best answered in simple economics. Remarkably, the question went unasked until recent research by Oregon fisheries economist Hans Radtke. Historically, hatchery managers have been overly optimistic about survival rates. In fact, survival rates for hatchery-raised fish are stunningly low, especially when compared with rates for naturally spawned fish. As this became apparent, hatchery managers compensated by turning up the volume, releasing even more fish to yield a desired final number, which generally further suppressed survival rates as a result of competition. The net result: at present, an average of less than one percent of coho and chinook smolts released from hatcheries survive to adulthood. Radtke applied those survival rates against costs, both fixed and variable, to raise each young salmon, then set those against average harvest rates to find that each harvested hatchery fish costs about $62.50 to produce. A fisherman who catches a hatchery fish sells it for considerably less than half that amount. Hatchery salmon now account for about thirty percent of all salmon produced worldwide, most of which come from the North Pacific.

These numbers help make sense of the emergence of criticism of the hatchery program from quarters beyond the usual environmental protests over the welfare of the fish. For instance, a report commissioned by the Oregon Business Council called the hatchery program a failure, in that despite its best efforts, salmon stocks were extinct or at least in deep trouble in precisely those areas — the southern half of the region — where hatcheries had been most active. The report's authors wrote: "While the machine model was ineffective, it has not been inexpensive. Prior to 1980, the salmon program, which was originally set for $20 million, consumed about $400 million and in the next ten years, $1.2 billion was spent."

These numbers are sufficiently large to attract a pro-business group's attention, and Radtke's fundamental calculations lie at the base of them. Behind these numbers, however, lies a fact even more fundamental than markets. Radtke also applied those survival rates to average weights of hatchery-reared salmon. His calculations showed that hatcheries dump more biomass into the system as juveniles than the biomass returned by spawning adults. Hatcheries have reversed the

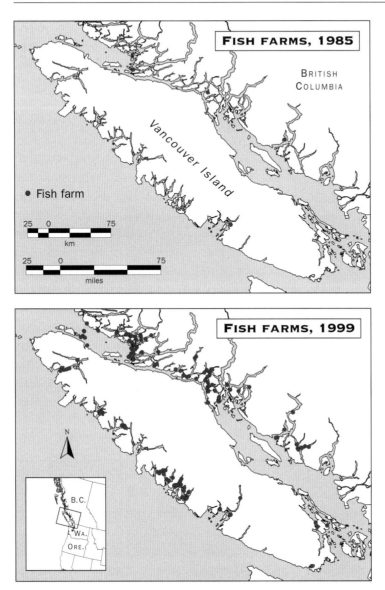

CLUSTERS OF FISH FARMS POSE RISKS TO SALMON RUNS NEAR VANCOUVER ISLAND

Salmon farms face criticism for their local environmental impacts: Concentrated fish excreta and uneaten fish meal flow right into the water from net pens, non-native Atlantic salmon periodically escape into Pacific waters, and fish farmers kill sea lions and seals that try to eat the penned fish. Under pressure from environmentalists and some First Nations, the Province of British Columbia imposed a moratorium on new fish farms in 1995, but lifted it in September 2002. Applications for at least twenty new farms are pending. In addition, a handful of farms are located in nearby Puget Sound, in Washington state waters.

Map by David Carruthers (Ecotrust Canada) based on data from the BC Ministry of Fisheries.

design of the system: they cause fish to export land-derived energy to the sea, instead of importing it from the pastures of the North Pacific to support communities like Namu.

Thirty percent of the world's salmon now come from hatcheries, but wild fish account for only another twenty to thirty percent. Almost all of those wild fish come from waters around Alaska and British Columbia, northern waters where runs are mostly intact. These are the waters from which we harvest volumes comparable to those native people caught for thousands of years, that is, in those places largely unmanaged. The biggest share of the world's salmon consumption, however — now forty to fifty percent — comes from farmed fish, salmon raised and fed artificially in net pens their entire lives. Salmon farming, or aquaculture, is the system's other big machine.

The rise of salmon farming worldwide helps explain the puzzling paradox in the economic picture. We understand that salmon runs are troubled, even endangered in some places. Scarcity ought to dictate a high price, yet salmon fishermen, especially in recent years, have faced catastrophically low prices. Chinook salmon, for instance, have fallen from $5 a pound in the seventies to as little as $1 now. In recent years, Alaskan waters have been producing well, an increase in supply that is one factor in the low price, but not the dominant one. The biggest factor is that fish farming is flooding the market. In 1980, farmed salmon accounted for about 1 percent of all production, yet now we see it approaching fifty percent and climbing. The boom in farming has largely occurred in Norway, Scotland, and Chile, but is gaining a firm foothold in Washington's Puget Sound and north along the southern B.C. coast in the waters surrounding Vancouver Island.

Like the hatchery boosters who preceded them, the fish farmers tell us aquaculture is good because artificially raised fish take pressure off the beleaguered wild stocks and at the same time provide a hungry world with more food. Environmentalists have countered that the farms pollute, and that escapees (mostly Atlantic salmon) spread disease to and compete with wild runs. The environmentalists are right, but set aside their argument for a second. This is not, as the farmers would have it, a matter of a conflict between the environment and the economic realities of feeding the world. Salmon farming fails the economic test as well.

BEHIND THAT FARMED SALMON STEAK

It's tempting: salmon fillets in the supermarket seafood case for just $3.99 a pound. Or a salmon entrée on the menu at a chain restaurant for under $10. This at a time when salmon catches are erratic from British Columbia southward, and you might have expected scarcity to have driven up the price. The explanation is simple: a glut of farmed fish — amounting to roughly half the world's supply of salmon — has flooded the market. Farmed salmon are raised in net pens in a number of cold-water locations, including Norway, Scotland, Chile, Washington state, and British Columbia. But the ingredients in a farmed salmon steak are quite different than what goes into its free-ranging cousins captured by nets or hooks. Take a look:

THE STRAIGHT POOP

The excreta from one large B.C. fish farm are estimated to equal the sewage of a city of ten thousand people — all of it flowing straight into the surrounding waters, fouling nearby clam beds and other sea habitat, at too high a concentration to be assimilated easily by natural forces. The David Suzuki Foundation estimates feces emissions at more than 40 percent of the live weight of the fish raised in pens — so an eight-ounce salmon steak represents a pile of feces about as big as the scoop of rice placed next to it on the plate. Salmon excreta are one reason that environmental activists are pushing for fish to be raised only in closed-containment systems, allowing the wastes to be treated before being discharged into the water. A recent B.C. ruling will allow ten such farms to be established in the province — where they will still be outnumbered by traditional farms ten-to-one.

NETTING PETER TO FEED PAUL

Salmon are carnivores. In captivity, they are raised on a diet of oily brown fishmeal pellets made from inexpensive fish such as anchovetas, sardines, and mackerel. To grow each pound of farmed salmon takes four pounds of those smaller fish, reducing the quantity of edible fish protein by 75 percent. In this way, B.C. farms alone account for a loss of nearly 90 thousand tons of protein each year.

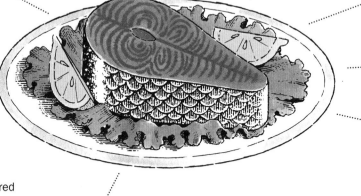

ALIENS ON THE LOOSE

Atlantic salmon have become a favorite of West Coast fish farmers, in part because they can be raised at higher densities than native chinook. These fish frequently escape from their pens into the wild. In 1997, one Washington state farm lost 360,000 Atlantic salmon in a single incident. Alien Atlantic salmon have been found to spawn successfully in Vancouver Island streams, and fishery advocates are concerned that they will compete with threatened populations of native Pacific salmon.

TRACKS LEADING IN, BUT NO TRACKS LEADING OUT

Most net pens are located in inlets, on the migration routes of many fish to and from their spawning grounds. Salmon are natural-born predators, so smaller fish that stray into the farms, including juvenile wild salmon, don't stand a chance. Salmon farmers notice that when young oolichan (minnow-sized smelt) pass by the pens, the salmon stop eating their fishmeal pellets but "mysteriously" continue to gain weight. The net pens are illuminated at night; farmed fish snap up the herring attracted by the lights.

MY, HOW PINK YOUR STEAKS ARE!

The better to fool you, my dear. Wild salmon flesh gets its color from the fish's prey, particularly krill, tiny shrimp-like crustaceans. But farmed fish eat pellets of fishmeal which would leave their flesh a pale gray instead. Fish farmers know that gray salmon won't sell well, so they add a dye called astaxanthin to their feed.

SALMON ON DRUGS

Farmed fish are so densely confined that a typical one-pound Atlantic salmon is within fifteen inches of its neighbors. Diseases can spread rapidly through such packed quarters, so the fish are fed antibiotics including oxytetracycline and sulfa drugs, just like most domestic chickens or cattle. About 30 percent of the medicated feed goes uneaten; from uncontained net pens it enters the sea's food chain, where it has been found to kill natural marine algae and bacteria and cause deformities in halibut larvae.

Nonetheless, the farmed fish still contract infections and parasites. Wild stocks pick up those diseases in two ways — either from escapees, or as they pass by the fish farms en route to or from their spawning streams. Norwegian authorities have opted to poison twenty-four rivers with rotenone — which kills all aquatic life — in an attempt to eradicate sea lice and a lesion-causing disease spread there by farmed salmon.

THEY SHOOT SEALS, DON'T THEY?

When seals see fish farms, they think "free lunch." To control their losses, fish farmers shoot seals that frequent their farms, killing an average of five hundred per year in British Columbia in the early 1990s. They also try to scare them off with "acoustic deterrent devices," which emit a screamingly loud underwater sound. That racket also keeps orcas and humpback whales far at bay, excluding them from valuable habitat.

Written by S. Zuckerman based on *Net Loss: The Salmon Netcage Industry in British Columbia* by David W. Ellis and Associates (Vancouver, B.C.: the David Suzuki Foundation, 1996) and on personal communications with Suzuki Foundation staff.

Does salmon farming take pressure off wild stocks? A commercial fisherman is not so much interested in the number of fish caught as the total income the catch generates. If a fisherman gets one-fifth the amount per fish, he must catch five times as many to maintain income, which regulations, of course, forbid. So there is increasing pressure on the regulations, increasing violation of them, and more broke fishers than there were a decade ago.

Yet this supply-demand-price haggle is but a small part of this picture, a narrow view of economics. Despite what you may have heard in the incessant jobs-versus-environment debate, biology respects an economic logic, ordering its market with the food chain. Species use resources according to their position in the chain. The chain serves no free lunch, particularly a free protein lunch, which is to say the protein of a farmed salmon does not come out of thin air. Animals low on the food chain eat plants. Cows eat carbohydrates in grass to make protein. Animals higher on the chain eat animals; they eat protein to make protein, losing as much as 90 percent of it in the process of maintaining life forces. This is why we don't, as a rule, raise predators for food.

But we do farm salmon, and salmon are predators; they eat fish. Estimates of the metabolic loss vary, but there is always a loss. For instance, the Worldwatch Institute says it takes about five grams of fish protein—converted into fishmeal—to make a gram of farmed fish protein. Fishmeal is produced globally, especially from sardines and anchovies of South America and especially from herring from the North Pacific.

Worldwide, salmon aquaculture is sponsoring a secondary fishery that vacuums the ocean floor like a Shop Vac. Ocean fisheries historically have been damaging enough to the environment, but were typically at least somewhat selective to marketable species. However, when the end product is fishmeal, virtually everything that shows up in a net can be ground into the mix, setting the stage for a decimation of the system the way pulpwood set the stage for clearcuts. Wild salmon know how to graze this ocean system selectively, efficiently harvesting its protein for us. Our blundering nets know only how to destroy it and move on.

Fish farming takes relatively low-cost protein, species once consumed directly by the world's poor, reduces its volume by a factor of five, and sells it to the world's wealthiest consumers. Meantime, wild fish, the few that are left, hatch to fingerlings and migrate to oceans only to find that the fishmeal trawlers have beaten them to their prey. This is the same logic that sent salmon fishers further to sea, but in this case, the trawlers are beating fish to fish, not other fishermen to fish.

We pay for this inefficient system in two ways. First, by relying upon a heavily capitalized, mechanized system that no longer uses the community labor of places like Namu. The system renders them redundant; they become ghost towns as the few jobs that remain move to factory trawlers and centralized processing plants.

Second, most of the cost of this Rube Goldberg machine that has replaced nature's intricate web comes by diminishing the productive capacity of nature. We live off the capital, not the interest. As market economists tell us, these are difficult costs to measure, these natural services that do nothing so much as make the world what it is. Difficult to measure, so we don't really feel the loss — until they are gone.

All of this converges on an emerging school of economic thought that seeks to assign dollar values to intact natural systems, a topic that has come to be known as "ecosystem services." The salmon offer a classic case. Pacific salmon gave us a primary product — food — but in the bargain, they imported nutrients sufficient to feed a whole system. That system, in turn, raised more fish, an ecosystem service to which we could easily assign a dollar value today simply by adding up the costs of the hatchery system that replaced it. Except that the natural system worked.

In considering Namu, though, it seems there was another, subtler, service at work.

Modern salmon politics are politics above all, spawning even cross-border diplomatic wars, seizures of vessels, lawsuits, and violence. All of this is about allocation. To read the headlines, one could believe that allocation is the sole problem of the salmon system. We committed ourselves to this path when we abandoned village-front fish traps and headed out to sea to try to beat other fishermen.

How much better did the salmon handle this job when allowed to return to their home streams? Their entire life cycle centered on a place. This was allocation, a system that assigned a volume of fish to a community, and in turn made the people who lived there responsible for maintaining the health of the watershed that would return that volume in all the years to come.

Salmon once sorted us into places like Namu, gave us fidelity to those places and a reason to protect them. Now we haven't the slightest notion how to do that for ourselves.

VAST AREAS HAVE LOST AT LEAST ONE SALMON RUN IN RECENT YEARS

Human activities have eliminated at least one run of salmon or steelhead trout in the watersheds shown in red. In all, 232 salmon stocks in the region are known to have been lost during the twentieth century. Extinctions are concentrated in the southern and eastern portions of the fishes' ranges, where human impacts have been most pervasive and the climate leaves salmon especially vulnerable to human-caused disruptions such as irrigation projects, logging, dam-building, and livestock grazing.

Range of Pacific salmon

Watersheds in which at least one salmon or steelhead stock extinction has been documented

100   0   300
miles

Map by Dorie Roth based on data from public sources

FOR THOUSANDS OF YEARS, COASTAL PEOPLES NOTED THE SALMON'S COMINGS AND GOINGS. IN NEW WAYS AND OLD, THE CURRENT INHABITANTS STILL DO. THE FOLLOWING PORTFOLIO REPRESENTS THE FIRST ATTEMPT TO COLLECT WHAT IS KNOWN ABOUT THE HEALTH OF PACIFIC SALMON STOCKS THROUGHOUT NORTH AMERICA. THESE MAPS OFFER CITIZENS OF SALMON NATION A VIEW OF THE WHOLE FROM A VANTAGE POINT IN THEIR OWN HOME WATERSHEDS.

PORTFOLIO

THE SIX SPECIES OF SALMON NATION

MAPS BY DORIE ROTH

Fisheries biologists divide the landscape

into "watersheds" (also known as "basins" or "drainages") — the area whose run-off flows into a particular stream. Because conditions all across a basin affect the watercourses that run through it, salmon are often said to live not just in streams, but in watersheds. Smaller drainages and their streams join together to form larger watersheds — for example, the Snake and Willamette joining with the Columbia. To make this mapping project manageable, large watersheds were broken into tributary watersheds, and small adjoining basins were considered together, in units that hydrologists refer to as "fourth-field watersheds." These are the areas that are each colored separately on the following maps. For some coastal areas, where the data are kept in finer detail, those finer divisions are used.

Often, several populations of salmon share each watershed. The West Coast of North America is home to five species of salmon (chinook, chum, coho, pink, and sockeye) and two species of sea-going trout (steelhead and cutthroat) that spawn in fresh water. The cutthroat trout does not undertake an extensive ocean migration, and was not included in these maps. Some species are further divided according to their season of spawning migration: fall-run chinook in a river are distinct from that river's spring run, as winter steelhead are from summer steelhead. A run of salmon or sea-going trout — composed of fish that are separated by species, timing, or geography from other groups of fish, and thus reproduce primarily with each other — is referred to as a "stock."

Stocks were rated according to a scale of health, from "low risk of extinction" through "at risk of extinction" (encompassing stocks judged to have either a moderate or high risk of vanishing) to "extinct." Some stocks, lacking definitive evidence for an at-risk rating, were classified as being "of special concern." These are populations that are susceptible to minor disturbances, are in danger of inter-breeding with large populations of hatchery fish, have some unique characteristic that sets them apart from neighboring stocks, or are apparently depleted but whose population trends are not well documented.

The data for these maps were collected from scientific papers, from public agencies such as the National Marine Fisheries Service and the Alaska Department of Fish and Game, and from studies by private non-profit organizations such as The Wilderness Society and Oregon Trout. Most of the data represent the state of the salmon as of the early to mid-1990s. In cases where different stocks of a particular species in a given watershed were rated differently, the watershed rating was assigned according to the status of the weakest stock in that basin.

For British Columbia and Alaska, information was more difficult to obtain than for the more southern parts of the salmon's range. Although state fisheries officials in Alaska do collect detailed information about the strength of their salmon runs, no systematic analysis of salmon populations across most of the state has been performed. In southeast Alaska, the only part of the state where that analysis was done, information was sufficient to determine trends in salmon populations for only one-tenth of the stocks. In British Columbia, many watersheds lack systematic information on salmon population because they are so remote.

Paired with the map for each species, you will find a summary of its current status under the U.S. Endangered Species Act. For this purpose, the National Marine Fisheries Service (NMFS) combines stocks into larger groupings known as "evolutionarily significant units." These are populations known to be genetically different enough from their neighbors to merit protection in the eyes of the law. For each species, the listing status is given as of March 2003. *Endangered* reflects the highest level of risk to the stock, with *threatened* indicating a stock on its way to "endangered" status if its decline is not arrested. *Candidate* stocks are still being evaluated for possible listing, and stocks marked as *not warranted* are those which in the agency's judgment do not qualify for listing — either because they are sufficiently robust or because they are already extinct. Updated information — and the exact boundaries of these Evolutionarily Significant Units — can be obtained from NMFS using contact information given in the Resources section on page 86.

ENDANGERED SPECIES ACT STATUS
AS OF MARCH 2003

ENDANGERED: upper Columbia spring run and Sacramento winter run

THREATENED: Snake fall and spring/summer run, Central Valley (Calif.) spring run, California coastal (south of the Klamath River), Puget Sound, lower Columbia, and upper Willamette

CANDIDATE: Central Valley (Calif.) fall and late-fall run

NOT WARRANTED: Deschutes, southern Oregon and northern California (between Oregon's Elk River and the Klamath River), Upper Klamath-Trinity, Oregon coast, Washington coast, middle Columbia spring run, and upper Columbia summer/fall run

CHINOOK
(also known as king, Tyee, or spring)

ONCORHYNCHUS TSHAWYTSCHA

Chinook runs have been increasing throughout Alaska. Commercial harvests are relatively high, though not as high as in the late 1970s and 1980s.

In much of British Columbia, escapement (the number of fish arriving at the spawning grounds) is declining, and seventeen stocks have been identified as extinct. On the Fraser River, however, escapement has been increasing, largely due to conservation measures initiated in the early 1980s.

Coastal stocks in Washington are listed as healthy, while Puget Sound stocks are declining, and five stocks are currently in critical condition. Along the Oregon coast, fall chinook runs are relatively stable except for declining runs in the southern region — a trend that continues down the California coast.

Large populations of chinook salmon once inhabited the drier interior regions, including the upper Columbia, Snake, and Sacramento-San Joaquin rivers. The majority of these runs are now extinct, while others are listed under the federal Endangered Species Act.

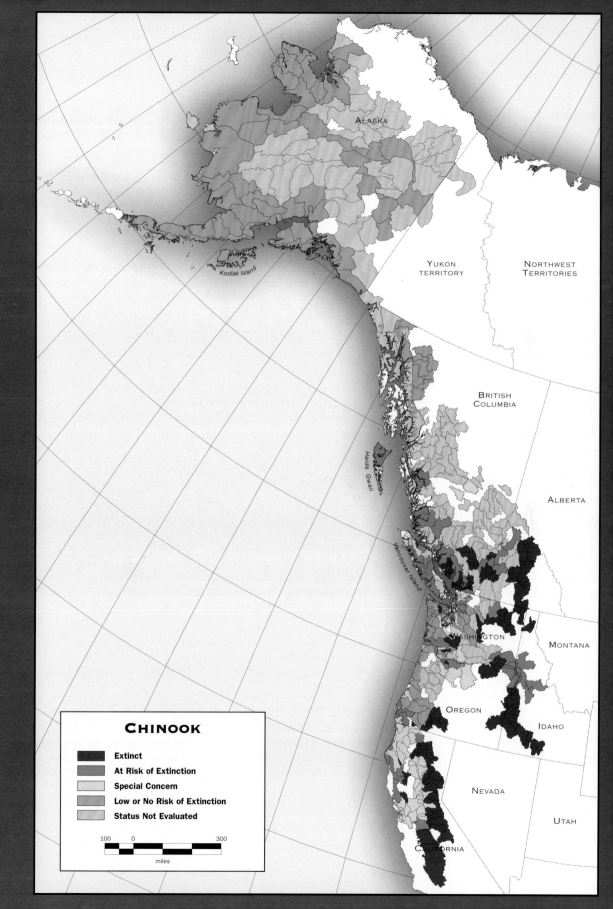

CHINOOK

- Extinct
- At Risk of Extinction
- Special Concern
- Low or No Risk of Extinction
- Status Not Evaluated

100   0   300

miles

CHUM
(also known as dog or keta)

ONCORHYNCHUS KETA

Catch levels of Alaskan chum are high, fluctuating around 15 to 20 million fish in recent years. Hatchery fish make up an increasing share of the commercial catch, amounting to more than one in four fish.

Of the 1,625 stocks identified in British Columbia, 141 (9 percent) were at high risk of extinction, and twelve stocks showed moderate risk. Most of the imperiled stocks occur in the Nass River, followed by basins on the north coast, Haida Gwaii (Queen Charlotte Islands), and the central coast. Of twenty-two chum stocks extinct in the province, seventeen had been found in the Vancouver area.

Most Washington chum runs are healthy, with the exception of two Puget Sound stocks in critical condition and lower Columbia River populations, which are declining. Chum are in critical condition in Oregon, where many populations are already extinct. Few chum remain in California.

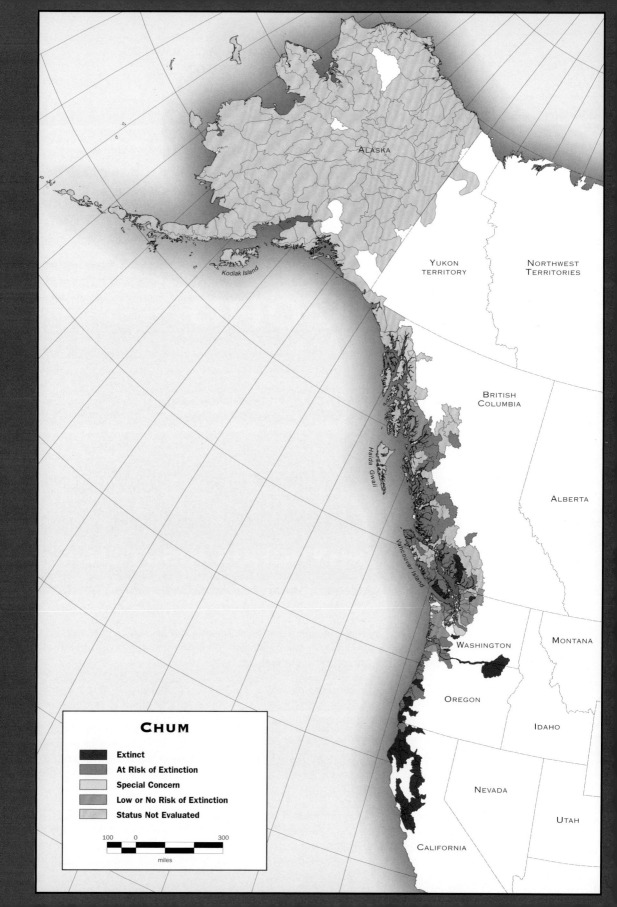

CHUM

Extinct
At Risk of Extinction
Special Concern
Low or No Risk of Extinction
Status Not Evaluated

ALASKA

Kodiak Island

YUKON
TERRITORY

NORTHWEST
TERRITORIES

BRITISH
COLUMBIA

Haida Gwaii

ALBERTA

Vancouver Island

WASHINGTON

MONTANA

OREGON

IDAHO

NEVADA

UTAH

CALIFORNIA

100   0   300

miles

THREATENED: Oregon coast, southern Oregon/northern California, and central California

CANDIDATE: Puget Sound/Strait of Georgia, lower Columbia/southwest Washington

NOT WARRANTED: Olympic Peninsula

COHO
(also known as silver)

ONCORHYNCHUS KISUTCH

In general, coho escapement (numbers of fish reaching the spawning grounds) is increasing throughout Alaska, with the exception of southeast Alaska. In recent years, Alaska has seen record commercial catches.

In British Columbia, coho runs are declining. By 1992, escapement had reached the lowest levels since the 1950s. Conservation measures put in place to protect coho have curtailed the B.C. commercial fishery and led to controversy over how many B.C.-bound salmon are intercepted by Alaskan fishing boats.

Most stocks along the Washington coast and in Puget Sound are rated as healthy. However, sixteen out of forty-six Puget Sound stocks were listed as depressed, and one was listed in critical condition.

Coho are now extinct in more than half of their historical range — in the upper Columbia and inland basins of Washington, Oregon, Idaho, and California. Nearly all remaining coho runs in Oregon and California are very small. Juvenile coho stay in fresh water for a year or longer, and are particularly vulnerable to habitat disruption.

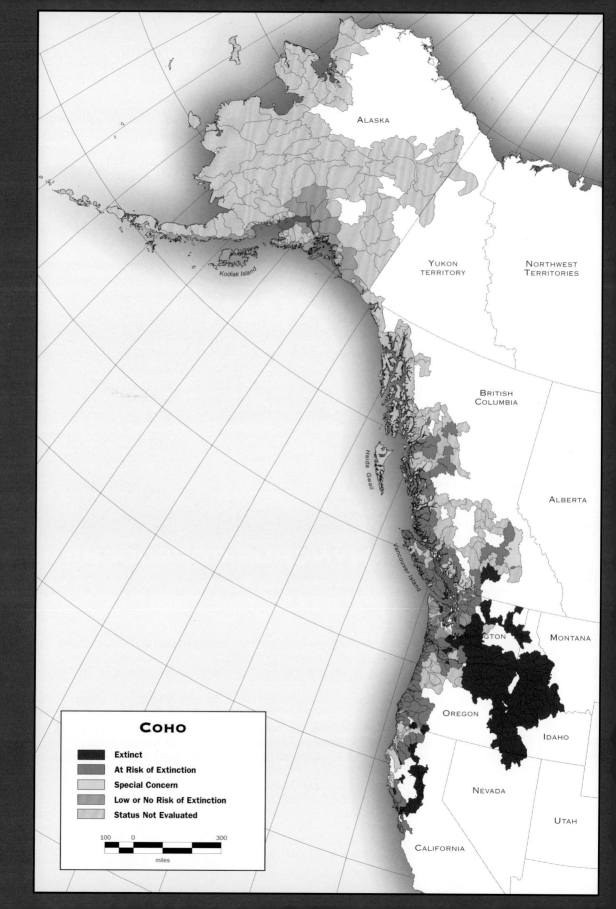

COHO

Extinct

At Risk of Extinction

Special Concern

Low or No Risk of Extinction

Status Not Evaluated

ALASKA

YUKON TERRITORY

NORTHWEST TERRITORIES

BRITISH COLUMBIA

ALBERTA

Kodiak Island

Haida Gwaii

Vancouver Island

WASHINGTON

MONTANA

OREGON

IDAHO

NEVADA

UTAH

CALIFORNIA

100   0   300

miles

ENDANGERED SPECIES ACT STATUS AS OF MARCH 2003

NOT WARRANTED: even-year and odd-year runs. (Pink salmon return to spawn after exactly two years. Thus, stocks that breed in even years are reproductively separate from those breeding in odd years.)

PINK
(also known as humpie)

ONCORHYNCHUS GORBUSCHA

In Alaska, catches of pink salmon have reached record levels, and escapement (numbers of fish reaching their spawning grounds) has been increasing as well. More than a quarter of the commercial catch in Alaska is the product of hatcheries.

On the Fraser River, escapement by pinks has risen from less than 1 million at the beginning of the 1990s to more than 3 million today. For comparison, historic runs averaged 50 million fish. Pink salmon populations have also increased in other basins throughout British Columbia, except in the vicinity of the Broughton Archipelago, where sea lice spread from salmon farms devastated the run in 2002.

In Washington, nine out of fourteen Puget Sound pink stocks are considered healthy, while two are in critical condition. One run, on the Elwha River, is considered extinct.

Self-sustaining populations of pink salmon apparently never occurred in Oregon. All California pink runs have become extinct.

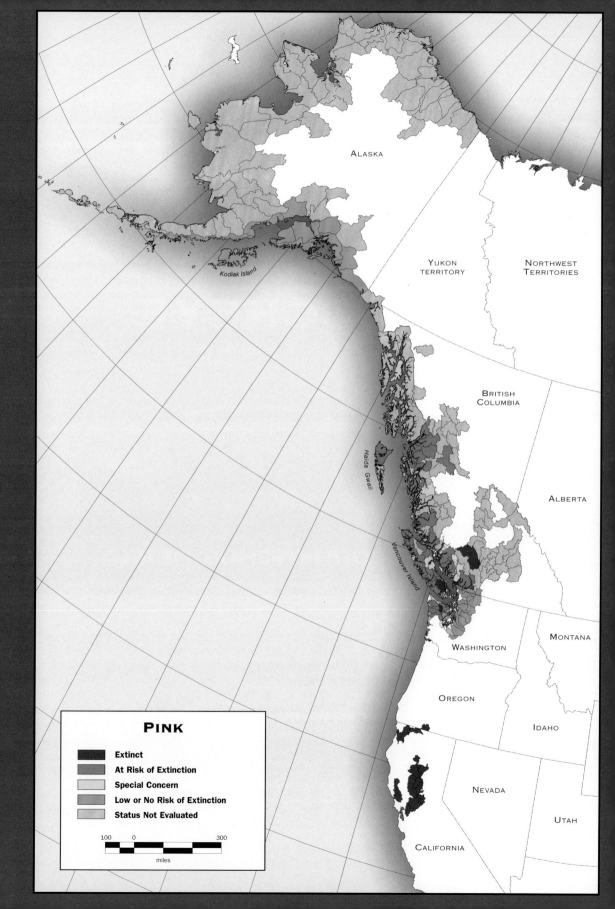

PINK

- Extinct
- At Risk of Extinction
- Special Concern
- Low or No Risk of Extinction
- Status Not Evaluated

100 0   300
miles

ALASKA

YUKON
TERRITORY

NORTHWEST
TERRITORIES

BRITISH
COLUMBIA

ALBERTA

Kodiak Island

Haida Gwaii

Vancouver Island

WASHINGTON

MONTANA

OREGON

IDAHO

NEVADA

UTAH

CALIFORNIA

ENDANGERED SPECIES ACT STATUS AS OF MARCH 2003

ENDANGERED: Snake River

THREATENED: Ozette Lake (Washington)

NOT WARRANTED: Baker River, Okanogan River, Lake Wenatchee, Quinault Lake, Lake Pleasant (all in Washington)

SOCKEYE
(also known as red)

ONCORHYNCHUS NERKA

Alaskan sockeye runs have varied in recent years, with the Bristol Bay run falling far short of expectations in 1997 and 1998, and rebounding in 1999. Trends of escapement (fish reaching their spawning grounds) have increased elsewhere in the state, except in southeast Alaska.

In British Columbia's Fraser River, sockeye escapements have risen in the past decade from 1.5 to 2 million fish — a figure that pales next to historic runs that may have reached 100 million fish. Sockeye numbers elsewhere in the province have also increased in recent years.

Runs of sockeye in the Columbia and Snake rivers are severely depleted or have been completely destroyed. Puget Sound sockeye declined in the 1990s, although a few runs have rebounded in response to restoration efforts. On the Washington coast, sockeye status ranges from healthy to at risk.

With the exception of a few sockeye that return to the Deschutes River in Oregon, there are no longer self-sustaining populations of sockeye in Oregon or California.

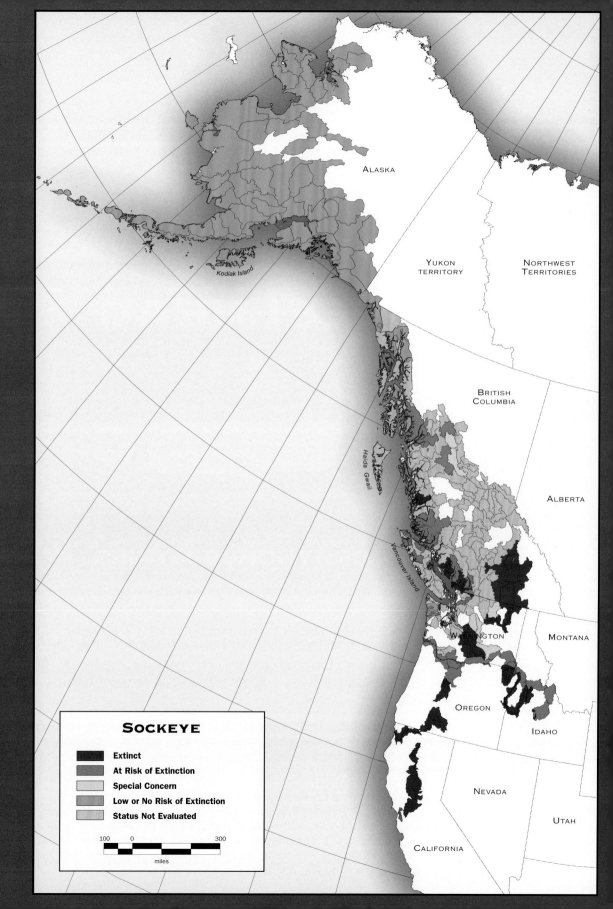

SOCKEYE

- Extinct
- At Risk of Extinction
- Special Concern
- Low or No Risk of Extinction
- Status Not Evaluated

100 0   300

miles

ALASKA

Kodiak Island

YUKON
TERRITORY

NORTHWEST
TERRITORIES

BRITISH
COLUMBIA

Haida Gwaii

Vancouver Island

ALBERTA

WASHINGTON

MONTANA

OREGON

IDAHO

NEVADA

UTAH

CALIFORNIA

ENDANGERED SPECIES ACT STATUS
AS OF MARCH 2003

ENDANGERED: southern California and upper Columbia

THREATENED: upper Willamette, middle Columbia, northern California, south-central California coast, central California coast, Snake River, lower Columbia, and Central Valley (Calif.)

CANDIDATE: Oregon coast

NOT WARRANTED: southwest Washington, Puget Sound, Olympic Peninsula, and Klamath Mountains

STEELHEAD

ONCORHYNCHUS MYKISS

Data on Alaskan steelhead stocks are sparse. Only two out of 336 identified stocks were well enough documented that their status could be evaluated. Both appeared stable.

About 40 percent of steelhead stocks in British Columbia are of special concern or at risk of extinction.

Winter and summer steelhead populations in Puget Sound have declined, primarily due to habitat damage. With a few exceptions, Washington coastal stocks appear to be healthy. Stocks that once inhabited the upper Columbia, Spokane and Pend Oreille rivers are now extinct.

Stocks along the Oregon and California coasts are in critical condition, with escapements declining. These declines have been attributed to poor ocean conditions, predation, habitat damage, and widespread operation of hatcheries. In the southern and inland portions of the steelhead's range, its situation is dire. Stocks in the interior basins of Oregon and California have become extinct largely due to dams, water diversion, and habitat damage.

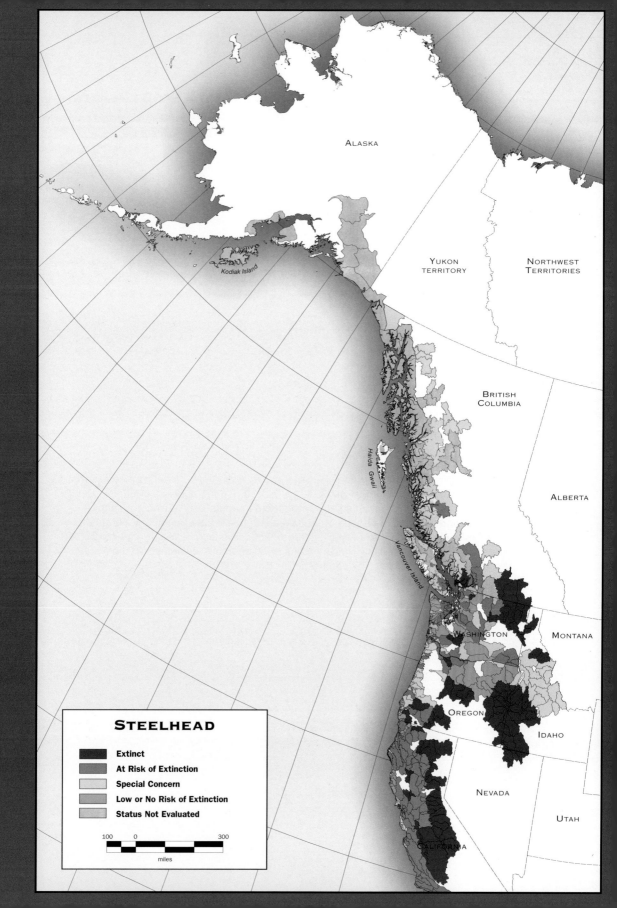

STEELHEAD

- Extinct
- At Risk of Extinction
- Special Concern
- Low or No Risk of Extinction
- Status Not Evaluated

100   0   300

miles

KEY TO THE HEALTHIEST STOCKS AND STREAMS OF OREGON AND WASHINGTON

Numbered approximately from north to south on facing page

Washington Rivers

1. Skagit River
2. Sauk River
3. Snohomish and Skykomish Rivers
4. Wenatchee River
5. Eld Inlet
6. Totten Inlet
7. Quillayute and Bogachiel Rivers
8. Hoh River
9. Queets River
10. Lewis River
11. Hanford Reach of the Columbia River

Oregon Rivers

12. Kilchis River
13. Wilson River
14. Trask River
15. Tillamook River
16. Nestucca River
17. Little Nestucca River

Healthy stocks depicted on the facing page include salmon and steelhead stocks that are at least two-thirds as abundant as would be expected in the absence of human impacts. These stocks also met two additional criteria: their populations have not recently declined, and they do not depend on hatcheries to bolster their numbers. For a full description of the survey and analysis, see Charles Huntington, Willa Nehlsen, and Jon Bowers, "A Survey of Healthy Native Stocks of Anadromous Salmonids in the Pacific Northwest and California," *Fisheries*, Vol. 21, No. 2, 1996.

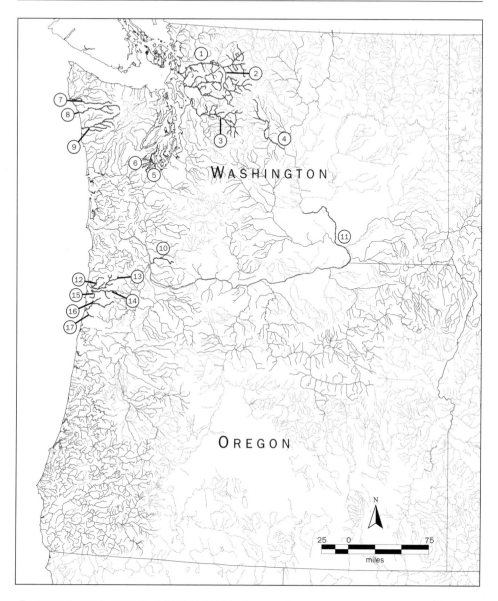

A FEW SALMON RUNS REMAIN STRONG AND HEALTHY

Amid the declining and endangered runs in Washington and Oregon, a few populations are still going strong. In 1993-95, a team of fisheries biologists compiled a list of those states' healthiest salmon and steelhead stocks, based on a survey of knowledgeable scientists. Three-quarters of the 99 healthy wild stocks they identified (including one in California) are chum, fall-run chinook, and winter steelhead. Streams highlighted on this map are home to the healthiest wild fish runs that the study found; they contain stocks at least two-thirds as abundant as would be expected in the absence of human impacts.

————— Streams with healthy runs

————— Salmon-bearing streams

Map prepared by Dorie Roth.

Freeman House has organized a significant part of his life around salmon. As a restoration activist on the Mattole River near his home in northern California, he has been a leader in articulating new-old ways to connect with the fish, the landscape and waters they inhabit, and the neighbors who share that place. In this essay, adapted from his book Totem Salmon, House offers insight into how his experiences as a commercial fisherman led him to that work.

Chapter 4

Keep the Gift Moving

BY
Freeman House

There is a hard knot of relationship in the

act of killing a creature of another species. It is an act that dissolves the illusion of individuality, of separateness. Perhaps this explains the terror that attends each such occasion, the awe that has inspired rituals and regulations, ceremonies and prayers in all human cultures throughout the ages. We are reminded in the most immediate way of our own mortality, an idea with which we may or may not have come to terms.

Modernity has distanced us from wild reality so that when it comes to killing and dying, each of us must deal with the mystery of it alone and uneasy. But the meaning persists in experiences of killing and dying, beyond cultural interpretation. The lesson of interpenetration is always available to us, regardless of our cultural conditioning. It is also a lesson we humans seem to be increasingly happy to ignore as we allow distant and abstract economic institutions to disguise and conceal the relationship. Could the food we buy in pretty shrink-wrapped packages ever have been alive as we are alive?

I am thinking of a moment in my life more than twenty-five years past, a moment that I have never fully comprehended. It was my second or third day out of Ketchikan, Alaska, as crew on a salmon purse seiner. In the Pacific Northwest, the purse seine has its origins in prehistory, in long, shallow nets made from twine woven painstakingly from the fiber of wild iris leaves, from cedar bark, from wild hemp, from willow bark. These nets, with a smaller mesh than others used to entangle the gills of fish, might be sixty to a hundred and fifty feet long, six to twenty feet deep. Making such a net was a communal endeavor that must have taken weeks, months: fibers no longer than the length of a forearm were twisted into long loops of cord, which were then woven and tied into large nets with an exactly measured mesh. (The knot used to tie the mesh five thousand years ago is the same one used today, the ubiquitous sheet-bend.) One end of the net was anchored to shore in deep but quiet waters. The other end was towed out by a canoe, then towed back to shore to form a circle. The net was weighted with rocks to hold down its bottom while wooden floats kept its top edge on the surface of the water. As the ends of the net were pulled ashore the circle became ever more constricted and the fish crowded within it were delivered to fishers with dip nets or spears. Versions of this sort of beach seine are still used by subsistence fishers in the inland waterways of British Columbia and Alaska.

With the arrival of the Euro-American commercial fishery in northwest North America, the old technology was adapted to deeper water, and eventually to diesel-powered boats. The nets, constructed now by clever machines, have grown to a quarter of a mile long and fifty feet deep. Polystyrene floats and lead-weighted lines have replaced wood and stone. Brass rings were added to the bottom of the net, through which a line is passed. The net is towed into its pretty circle by a skiff only slightly less powerful than the mother ship. Then, when the line running through the rings at the bottom of the net is winched on board, it closes off the whole expanse of water inside the net, along with all the life within it, like the drawstrings on a pouch, the purse seine.

For many years, the large nets were then drawn on board the mother boats by men straining with all their strength against the weight and pull of the water. (To the deckhands, it can't have seemed much of an improvement over the older native practices, which in my mind I see as leisurely and festive events.) In the days before sonar fish-finders and carefully coded radio transmissions, finding the schools of salmon that triggered the setting of the net depended on the hard-earned skills of the skipper, skills based on experience and observation. It was a calling to which the best of them devoted a life. Experience taught them a sense of timing that combined the day of the year with water temperatures and local weather patterns. Anomalies in the way sea mammals and birds were acting were a language they learned to understand; a boil of her-ring or a congregation of birds spoke to them more clearly than did their wives on the too-rare occasions when they returned home.

The perfect set enclosed a few hundred acre-feet of water swarming with schools of salmon—innumerable small pink salmon, their numbers compensating for the low price dictated by their eventual processing into canned food for pets and poor people; chinooks, less abundant but huge, and cohos, sleek and firm, which brought a better price and were headed for regional dinner tables. The great prize was the beautiful red-fleshed sockeye, prime food delivered fresh or frozen to expensive restau-rants in distant capitals.

By 1973, an innovation had been added to purse-seine technology that increased its efficiency enormously—the power gurdy. A gurdy is a stationary pulley hung on a davit. On salmon trollers, which catch fish by hook and line, the davit holds the pulley out over the water away from the boat, to provide smooth passage for the fishing lines when they are being pulled in or let out by hand, or by hydraulically powered winches. On a purse seiner, the power gurdy is a large, hydraulically powered hard rubber reel, hung by steel beams twelve feet above the stern of the boat, large and powerful enough to haul in both ends of the purse seine and drop them onto the net platform below.

Now the net, weighing several tons, could be pulled on board mechanically, the large winch started and stopped by a remote push-button. The time it took to play out the net and pull it in was reduced to half an hour, increasing the number of sets that one crew could make in a day by a factor of four or more. The work of the crew changed from two hours of long, slow pulling to ten minutes of frenzy for a stern crew of three whose job it was to stack the incoming net under our feet at the same time as it was descending on our heads. We worked in full raingear with our sleeves and pantslegs taped shut against the stinging jellyfish and the enormous amounts of water. The occasional smaller gill-entan-gled fish was ignored.

GILLNETTER
Typical length 25 to 35 feet; average 30 feet.

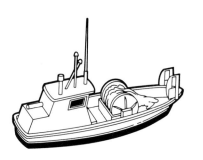 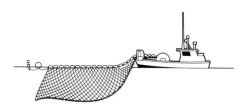

TROLLER
Typical length 35 to 65 feet; average 50 feet.

 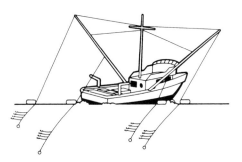

SEINER
Typical length 50 to 80 feet; average 70 feet.

 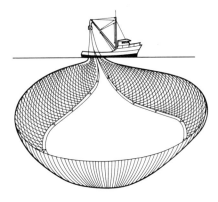

FIELD GUIDE TO COMMON FISHING VESSELS OF SALMON NATION

The boats on the facing page are the main types used in the North American salmon fishery. A **gillnetter** operates in inlets and rivers and near shore. It deploys a nearly invisible net in which fish become entangled, often caught by their gills when they swim into it. **Trollers** tow baited hooks through the water, and catch salmon sooner than the other boats, well before they enter the river to spawn. Trollers sometimes fish for other species such as albacore. **Seiners** use a small skiff to tow a net into a circle around a school of fish. The bottom of the net is cinched tight, trapping the fish from below. The net is then winched on board with its load of fish — a technology sometimes used for herring as well.

The two boats shown below are commonly seen at West Coast docks, although they are not used in the salmon fishery. **Trawlers** pull a net through the water, much as butterfly hunters use one. They target fish such as snapper and hake; some versions, known as factory trawlers, are much larger and process their catch at sea. **Longliners** seek bottomfish such as halibut by deploying baited hooks along a line that is then anchored to the seafloor. Some longliners, such as the one shown here, are rigged to troll as well. Other boats not shown include crab boats (look for crab pots on board) and oyster barges.

TRAWLER
Typical length 80 to 100 feet.

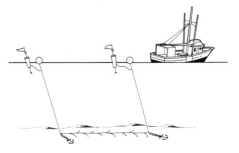

LONGLINER
Typical length 40 to over 100 feet.

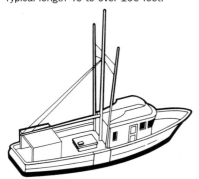

The independent skippers of these fishing boats had embraced the new machinery as the promise of their own survival in the fiercely competitive race to catch enough fish each year to make payments on the expensive new gear, to make mortgage payments on the house on shore, to keep food on the table for the kids. The new gear allowed them to catch more fish; the expense of the new gear required them to catch more fish. They were like caged squirrels on an exercise wheel.

For the crewman, the first challenge of the new machinery was simply to survive it. We were driven by the speed at which the power gurdy poured the bulk of the net down upon us. We worked in short bursts of incredible effort. It was the four-hundred-yard dash of fishing. We couldn't have moved any faster than the inexorable turn of the gurdy pushed us, and had the net been fifty feet longer it would have been an effort beyond our endurance. I was thirty-five years old, the oldest green member of the crew by a good ten years. The younger men on either side of me were of the type that rises full-hearted to challenges to their strength and stamina. Like athletes, they turned the challenge into art, a wild muscular dance. For my part, I thought only of trying to keep up with the younger men. The crew on the stern gave all their concentration and strength to meeting the demands of the machine. Sticks and twigs must be removed so as not to foul the net when racing to make the next set; if the power gurdy had to be stopped to remove debris, the skipper might fly into a rage. Keeping pace with the speed at which the seine came on board would for ten or fifteen minutes occupy every corner of consciousness, every fiber of muscle.

The moment of truth at the end of each set comes when the pocket at the bottom of the purse has been drawn in close to the boat, the remainder of the net stacked on board. If the men on the stern, the webmen, have performed well, this will be the first time the power gurdy has paused in its relentless turning. Now the whole crew — all seven of us — rushes to the side to see the size of the catch. Each one of us hopes to see the frenzied boil in the water that will tell us the catch is a big one, the payload that will make our day or our week. With the whine of the power winch stilled, the idling engine of the boat and the raucous scream of gulls are background noises that frame a moment frozen in time. The bunched floats bob and drift in the swell. Someone will break the curious stillness with a shout of "Payload!" if the net's pocket is full, or "Water haul" if, as happens more frequently, it is empty. Most often, twenty to a hundred salmon of various sizes circle languidly within the enclosure. One or another of them will be charging the seine, searching for a way out of the strange obstacle that has interrupted its migration. The net is full of motion and life; it is a cell isolated suddenly from the living plasm of the sea.

Two or three of the crew hold the top edges of the seine up out of the water with long boat hooks, an occasionally successful attempt to keep the jumpers inside. Two more gather the seine at the level of the rail and tie it tight with a line that is attached to a separate winch that will lift the bottom of the net with its captured fish on board. The power winch whines again, and the writhing cell of web and fish is hauled over the deck, pouring a ton of sea water as it comes up and is muscled on board.

A trip-line opens the purse, and the load of fish falls to the deck. They flop and writhe noisily, their tails pounding against the wooden deck. They are ignored or kicked aside as preparations for the next set are made. Only after the net is ready to be deployed into the water once more will a large hatch in the center of the stern deck be lifted so the fish can be put into the hold. They take a long time to die down there. Often, while we are hosing down the deck to clear it of seaweed and jellyfish, and the bolder seagulls are making runs at the flotsam, we can hear the fish drumming themselves to death below our feet, the sound amplified by the echo in the mostly empty space.

In retrospect, I can see that we were a perfect microcosm of an extractive industrial economy. The cannery owned and maintained the boat, which was leased to the skipper. The skipper owned the huge web of net, which had to be repaired daily and replaced entirely every two years or so at a cost of several thousand dollars. Boat, net, skipper, and crew each were recompensed by a share of the profits from the catch after fuel and food expenses had been taken off the top. Our livelihoods depended entirely on the size of the season's catch, and it was not impossible to work for four months of intermittent twenty-hour days and find oneself broke at the end of the fishing year. Each one of us was unthinkingly married to the goal of taking all the fish we could in the shortest time possible, and the pace and practice of our work was determined by the machinery we used. Under such conditions, the nature of what we were doing—taking life in order to feed ourselves—became obscure, if not lost altogether. We could not afford to see the creatures dying slowly on the deck and in the fish hold as manifestations of creation equal in complexity and vitality to ourselves.

We could only allow ourselves to see the salmon as objects, as product, a product that we hoped would allow us to pay the rent at home for a little longer than the duration of the fishing season.

This conditioning was reinforced by a collective psychology in the social pressure cooker of seven men isolated on a fifty-foot boat. It was a taboo all the stronger for remaining unspoken that the death of the fish was not to be discussed. Perhaps taboo is the wrong word, coming to us as an anglicized version of a Tongan word which can be translated as sacred. But the economic objectification of what we were doing was, in fact, violating something in us that does lie in the realm of the sacred: individuality disappears except as it can be defined in relation to the whole. By denying ourselves the perception of our relation to the creatures dying on deck, we were in some essential way denying ourselves a wholeness of being. And that knowledge lay large and dark and unarticulated just below the limited range of expression our condition allowed.

For non-Indian Americans too new to the land and waters of the Pacific Northwest to have developed ceremonies of place, the messages that salmon bring us are the same messages they have always brought, but they are not heard by most of us. Now — here — the message of the wild is fairly screaming at us in the midst of a deckload of slowly dying fish, but the message is carried at a different frequency than the one pulsing between the twin poles of our modern cultural icons of property and individualism. All of us on the boat speak English, and among us there is a smattering too of Norwegian, of Czech, of German — all languages which have been twisted over time into compliance with the dictates of economics and the physical sciences. None of us knows a word of Tlingit or Haida or Salish, languages that still resonate with the lives of salmon. Nevertheless, each of us retains some genetic memory — a memory embedded in our flesh — of the wild relationships out of which we have evolved. The demands of the power gurdy rob us of all but a dim and paradoxical remnant of direct engagement with the processes of life, with the genteel ethic of the clean kill — the expression of respect and compassion that recognizes the relationship between eater and eaten.

On the day I am thinking of, the lines have been carefully coiled and the stacked web checked to make sure it will flow out smoothly during the next set; the skiff is snubbed up close to the mother ship. The diesels roar at full bore as we take a position among the other purse seine boats to wait for the next set. Only now are the fish on deck given attention. Most of them are still vigorously alive, struggling and flopping against the alien media of full light and air. The crew react variously to the prospect of turning flesh into product. Some have leaped forward in their minds and are already calculating pounds and translating them into dollars; they do their work gleefully, shouting happily. Others sweep the fish into the hold tight-jawed and silent. One, a college boy/naturalist, had signed on to get close to ocean life-forms. Although no one has told him so, he knows as well as anyone that he dare not take the time to dispatch the fish respectfully and individually. He seems to go crazy, kicking the fish and shouting curses at them. I notice that he seems to be aiming the kicks of his steel-toed rubber boots at that spot behind the head of each fish that will kill it quickly.

I have no memory of having arrived where I did by any logical thought process; I don't remember telling myself that this is what I should do. But I found myself alone in a dark corner of the fish hold squatting with a ten- or twelve-pound sockeye salmon still alive across my knees. With a knife I opened up its chest cavity just enough to find the heart and tear it out with two fingers and a thumb. It came with a ripping and squirting sound. I popped the heart into my mouth and bit down once, hard, through the gristly thing. One bite brought a flavor like all of Icy Straits and enough saliva to float ten salmon hearts, enough to swallow it whole. As I swallowed, all my floating terrors gained a name and swept through me with the intensity of a hurricane. Fear of fish flesh and cold blood, fear of slime on the flesh of fish and its absence on the skin of snakes, fear of the strangeness of other species, fear of a world barren of human thought, fear of death: my own and all of it.

I was back on the deck minutes later; no one seemed to have noticed my absence. I resumed the drill of preparing for the next set with an unusual clarity of vision and emptiness of mind. The shards of light reflecting from the surrounding sea, the crazy screams of the gulls and terns, the fading colors of the dying fish, all took on the aspect of a single thought that may or may not have been my own.

Some years afterward I found this passage, written by David Abram:

Naturally then, the mountains, the creatures, the entire non-human world is struggling to make contact with us. The plants we eat or smoke are trying to ask us what we are up to; the animals are signalling to us in our dreams or in forests; the whole Earth is rumbling and straining to let us remember that we are of it, that this planet, this macrocosm is our flesh, that the grasses are our hair, the trees our hands, the rivers our blood, that the Earth is our real body and that it is alive.

I stayed on to finish the season and went home to Puget Sound with four thousand dollars in my pocket, more than I had ever made in an equivalent time before. I had managed—hundreds of times—to keep my feet out of the vicious coils of rope that could have pulled me into the killingly cold brine as they raced out with the net. I had also learned the ropes of the industrial hierarchy: it wasn't long before I had lobbied my way into the cook's job, which no one else wanted much anyway, so I no longer had to perform that mad dance stacking web on the stern. (During a set, the cook was the person who held the push-button box that stopped and started the power gurdy.) I had managed to not quite drink myself to death at the bars in Ketchikan and Hoonah and Petersburg during the intervals between four-day openings. At the end of the season I knew I wouldn't return; I ended my industrial fishing career muttering comparisons to the last of the buffalo hunters. From that point on I would do my killing for food one creature at a time.

I had gone west to make my fortune, like many others had before me. But I had found a great deal more than the wad of money that would keep me in the months to come. If the purse seine boat was a model of a commodity economy, salmon had shown me that it was floating in a sea of natural provision, the boundless generosity of the Earth. Salmon was but one of the more dramatic expressions of the gift of food, the gift of life. That revelation was itself a gift that would keep me forever if I could learn to translate the obligation it placed upon me. Lewis Hyde, in his priceless book *The Gift: Imagination and the Erotic Life of Property* has this to say about that obligation: "The gift that cannot be given away ceases to be a gift. The spirit of the gift is kept alive by its constant donation." The gift that does not continue to move, dies.

Years after my season on the purse seiner, I moved to a small homestead in northwestern California and became involved in community efforts to restore the Mattole watershed. In part, it was a half-conscious attempt to keep the gift moving. And, as Hyde also says, "the giving of gifts tends to establish a relationship between the parties involved." In our modest efforts to give a dwindling salmon run a second chance, my neighbors and I are bound to each other through our tentative and cautious engagement with the very processes of creation. We are related through direct engagement with a race of salmon.

On a mid-winter morning a few years after we began this work, newly fertilized salmon eggs have been tenderly placed in a simple incubation trough built with our own hands. Beside the creek we call Arcanum, after the name of the business run by the two potters who own the land, we are forging new relationships with our watershed neighbors, who will tend the eggs and their emergent fry, and with the children who will return them to the wild in a few months. Most importantly, we have begun our engagement with a place, a place defined by the waters of the river we work in, a place where we may yet come to be at home.

THE NEWS FOR SALMON ISN'T ALL BAD. EVEN IN THE FACE OF
SHRINKING SALMON RUNS, FALTERING FISH PRICES, AND INEFFICIENT
FISH-FARMING OPERATIONS, A RENEWED RELATIONSHIP BETWEEN
HUMANS AND SALMON IS BEING TESTED IN COMMUNITIES SCATTERED
ACROSS SALMON NATION. WRITER SETH ZUCKERMAN INTRODUCES
A FEW OF THE ARTISTS AND ACTIVISTS, ANGLERS AND ACTORS
WHO ARE CRAFTING THIS RELATIONSHIP.

CHAPTER 5

TOWARD A NEW
SALMON ECONOMY

BY SETH ZUCKERMAN

For all the troubles they face, salmon still

inhabit the soul of the Pacific Northwest. Even though humans play awkward midwives to many salmon — barging them around dams to reach the ocean, or slicing them open to incubate their eggs in plastic cages — the fish leave their imprint on the place where we live. In diminished numbers they nonetheless connect ocean denizens and land dwellers in a bond that has been recognized since the days of the first peoples. Just as salmon once brought food for bear, human, and fir tree to the furthest reaches of our watersheds, they tantalize today with the dream of a place in which people can harvest what we need and stand back while the rest of the wild fulfills its own destiny.

That dream of living with the salmon and healing the relations between our species has motivated hundreds of initiatives by citizen groups and entrepreneurs throughout the fish's range. It has spawned watershed councils, fish-rearing projects, and bronze sculptures, and led otherwise sedentary individuals to spend Saturdays pulling brush and planting trees. It has moved some fishermen to handle their fish like gifts instead of cargo, and fish-buyers to value the difference between a factory fish and a wild fish. These broad-based efforts offer the most hope that humans can again show respect for the salmon in the fabric of our way of life, and work out mutually beneficial terms for sharing the North Pacific basin with them. By doing so, we can begin to develop the principles for cooperation with one another and the rest of creation that will allow not only salmon but salamanders and spruce trees to make their way in the world on a fair footing with *Homo sapiens*.

I first became aware of this promising approach to salmon in 1984, when I visited the remote Mattole valley in northwestern California. The chinook and coho salmon runs in this 300-square-mile watershed were in steep decline, and state agencies had not made the Mattole a priority because it is a small river, sparsely inhabited and far from population centers.

Nonetheless, a small band of local residents determined to do what they could in hopes of bringing back the fish. The first problem they identified was the lack of clean spawning gravel: salmon lay their eggs in streambed nests (called "redds"), where they are kept alive by oxygen in the water that flows through the spaces between the stones. But in the Mattole (as in many other watersheds), mud eroding into the streams because of clearcut logging and careless roadbuilding was smothering the eggs before they could hatch. Resident salmon-keepers launched a small hatchery project to boost the eggs' chances of survival by incubating them in troughs supplied with clean water. They set hand-built traps in the river and tended them through winter storms, hoping to catch fertile adult salmon before the river rose too high for them to continue fishing. Unlike an industrial hatchery, they took only wild fish, and just a fraction of those. They didn't rebreed the offspring of their project if they caught them as adults, because they sought to provide an insurance policy against extinction, not to create a population forever dependent on human intervention.

I was captivated by the élan these inhabitants brought to their work and by their vision of renewed plenty in which salmon feed people and the spirit of the land. They weren't waiting for anyone to solve the problem for them, they were doing what they could to address it head-on. I visited as often as I could, making the six-hour drive from San Francisco over tortuous roads to a place where, I felt, the people and their enterprises were in the right proportion to the terrain.

For the Mattole's fish runs to become self-sustaining again, the spawning habitat would have to improve. That meant preventing new insults from being inflicted on the landscape, and helping the older ones to heal. So the Mattolians' work branched out to include mapping the old-growth forest that still sheltered the best spawning grounds and seeking to protect it; finding out where erosion was coming from and working to stanch it; locating barren old clearcuts and reforesting them. It was four years after my first visit that I moved to the Mattole and became a participant in this work, shouldering a planting hoe and hoisting bags full of Douglas-fir seedlings onto my hips to establish trees where none had grown back in twenty years.

Since then I have planted fir, redwood, and willow trees, taken part in early winter counts of spawning salmon, and surveyed the young fish migrating to the ocean in late spring. I have sat in council with fifty of my neighbors — ranchers and restorationists, fishing outfitters and foresters — as we determined that the coho and chinook runs in our river had dropped so low that we oughtn't be fishing for the time being. Concern for the fish brought us all together as nothing before or since. We unanimously asked the state Fish and Game Commission to close our river to anglers during salmon season, a request which the surprised commission granted. And I have watched in frustration when we landowners couldn't agree on measures to keep the watershed's recovery on track.

For each of our missed opportunities, I am inspired by groups elsewhere along the coast that have notched successes where we have failed. On the southern Oregon coast, lawyer-turned-organizer Anne Donnelly leads the Coos Watershed Association with great subtlety, working with large industrial landowners, public foresters and ranchers who between them control almost all of the basin's 600 square miles. She concluded early on that little was to be gained by forcing people to protect the streams and fish runs if they didn't want to. "A lot of [the practices that harm the fish are] a matter of local custom," she says. "We're trying to effect cultural change, and you don't do that with a stick." Instead, Donnelly has organized field trips so landowners can hear from outside

WATERSHED RESTORATION GROUPS HAVE SPREAD THROUGH THE NORTHWEST

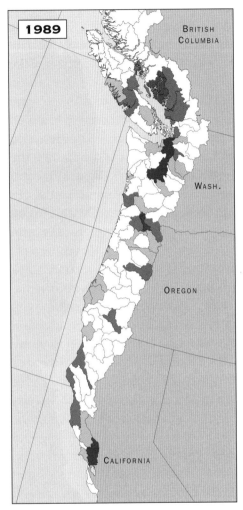

Rising with the tide of public concern for salmon and the watersheds they inhabit, the number of civic groups organized to protect and restore the fishes' habitat continues to grow. These maps show the rapid growth in the formation of such groups in the area west of the Cascade Range, from 94 in 1989 to 369 in 2002. In Oregon, this growth has been driven in part by a state-sponsored drive to organize watershed councils.

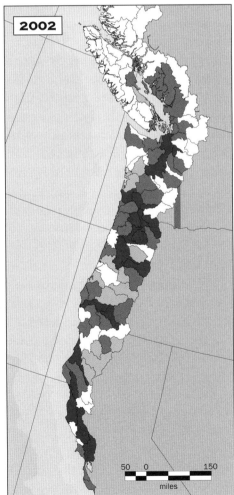

Number of watershed and restoration groups, by drainage or group of drainages

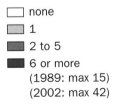

□ none
▨ 1
▩ 2 to 5
■ 6 or more
(1989: max 15)
(2002: max 42)

Map by Debra Sohm and Andrea Hildebrand based on a telephone survey.

experts what makes a culvert impassable to fish, for example, and find out what can be done about it. She also brought in crews to help timber companies spot places where their roads were bleeding sediment into the creeks during winter storms. A few years into the effort, she is starting to see the effects, both through projects to improve habitat with private and public funds, and through changes in how companies like Weyerhaeuser maintain their roads. "The most cost-effective way to do things is to create a social climate in which people do it themselves," says Donnelly. "I'm trying to get these guys to want to do the right thing."

Peppered up and down the coast are groups like the Mattole's and the Coos's that have arisen to aid the region's faltering fish populations, coalitions rather different than those formed around endangered creatures that people don't typically catch and eat, such as the marbled murrelet, the northern spotted owl, or the Olympic salamander. From Porcher Island off Prince Rupert, B.C., to Port Townsend, Wash., and Briceland, Calif., residents are raising fish in streamside hatchboxes. They are cabling logs into creekbeds to provide shelter to fish, buying irrigation rights to put water back into streams in dry summer months, and fencing livestock away from streambanks which then revegetate and offer shade and protection to juvenile fish. Each river — each pool and riffle — is unique, and teaches us that there is no one way to save salmon. This work challenges us to discover the particulars of our home-place and our fish, and adjust our actions to their needs.

The support of salmon is not merely a rural pursuit. In cities from San Francisco to Vancouver, neighborhood associations are trying to keep remnant fish runs alive, or to resuscitate populations pushed over the brink by the destruction of their habitat. Under pressure from urban activists, creeks formerly encased in storm sewers have been "daylighted" — exposed to the sun and air again, meandering between replanted banks. Steep culverts have been equipped with baffles to allow adult fish to migrate upriver in the face of torrential flows that would otherwise flush them downstream. And spawning populations, once taken for granted and largely ignored, have begun to be celebrated.

The effects are beginning to be felt, not only in the modest impact on the numbers of fish, but in the attachment to place that the fish awaken in people. Whether you live in the tiniest village or the largest metropolis, you live in a watershed, an area whose run-off flows via a network of streams through one outlet into a larger body of water such as a river, bay, or ocean. If that watershed drains more than a couple of garden hoses' worth into the North Pacific, at least one of the six species of Pacific salmon is probably native to it. A concern with salmon transforms residents of Fremont, Calif., into inhabitants of the Alameda Creek watershed, alert to the activities and phenomena there which affect the fish with whom they share the neighborhood. It helps when, as at Willamette Falls outside of Portland, or beside Ballard Locks in Seattle, city-dwellers can watch as the fish struggle to make their way upstream.

Concern for the fish isn't just about muddy work and political organizing. The annual return of the fish is occasion for celebration, as nourishing for the soul as their flesh is for the body and as their carcasses are for the streams and forests. One group that understands this more than most is Wild Olympic Salmon in Chimacum, near Port Townsend, Washington. Since 1989, these salmon aficionados have held a Wild Olympic Salmon festival every other autumn to mark the fish's return. Complete with pageantry, theater, and fish barbecue, the festival is a way for local residents to fête the salmon as they return to spawn.

Two of the founders of the festival, Tom Jay and his wife Mall Johani, are visual artists and carry the same fishy focus into their art as well. Jay's cast bronze sculptures are found all over the Northwest. In the Chimacum area, one of the most striking is Heroic Chum, a chum head bursting forth out of the earth in the parking lot of a strip mall and symbolizing the return of the fish. Johani's work tends more toward folk art —salmon-shaped throw pillows, glass beads in the form of a salmon egg, and even a curved Australian-style throwing stick with the legend "Salmon Come Back," which she calls a "salmorang". The couple's most ambitious project is yet to be realized: a 500-foot-long outline of a salmon drawn in oyster shell on a treeless hill across from the airport. "It would mark this forever as a place of salmon," Johani says.

Salmon biologists tell us that the unique characteristics of each place shape the life history of each population of fish. Chinook are known as spring salmon in much of their northern range because that is when they return to spawn. But in the coastal streams of California, they don't enter the streams until the freshets of fall signal the beginning of the rainy season. On the Columbia, one run of chinook was known as "June hogs" because of their mammoth size — up to 100 pounds — which enabled them to endure a thousand-mile upriver migration to the headwaters of the Columbia in Canada. Even within my own tiny watershed, the fall-running chinook spawn some young that swim out to the ocean in the spring and others that exit to the ocean after spending their first summer in the estuary.

Wherever fish-centered culture occurs, it too has an equally distinct local flavor. Long nights on the salmon trap in the Mattole spawned a series of songs about the fish and the humans awkwardly trying to help them. "I'm the queen of the pool, queen of the river," proclaims a female chinook in a doo-wop tune. "This is my valley, here's where my heart's at home," sings a well-meaning logger. Spurred on by talent shows on rainy winter evenings, the songs became skits and eventually a full-blown musical comedy, *Queen Salmon*, which toured the Northwest three times in the early to mid-'90s.

For as long as people have made art about salmon and for much longer than they have been restoring fish habitat, people have been eating salmon. That visceral connection—all of us who have eaten that pink flesh are at some molecular level part-salmon—makes many of us care about these fish even more than other endangered species. We sense that if the fish are in trouble, so are we, that their disappearance threatens to evict us from an Eden in which wild protein made its way to us on a regular basis.

It came as a shock to many inhabitants of the North Pacific Rim to learn that some salmon stocks were seriously depleted. Several groups found the news of particular concern: commercial fishers, anglers and their guides, and native peoples who have depended on these fish for thousands of years. Their responses vary. Early reactions tend toward blame: fishers condemn their colleagues who use different kinds of gear, whose ships fly different flags, or whose skin is a different color. Shifting weather patterns and deep-sea trawl and drift-net fisheries are often cited, and no discussion of salmon decline is complete without pointing a finger or a 30-30 at sea lions. Their anger comes from an understandable sense of loss: As recently as the late 1970s, commercial ocean salmon fishing in Washington, Oregon and California brought in an average annual catch valued at $180 million, and was responsible for 7,200 jobs in fishing, fish processing, and supporting industries. By 1997, estimates fisheries economist Hans Radtke, the income generated by the ocean catch had dropped to $26 million, and about six thousand jobs had been lost. But after tempers cool and reality settles in, people of a constructive bent try to salvage what they can and adapt their fishing to the current situation in which farmed fish glut the market while wild stocks face an uncertain prospect.

The perversity of the global economy is that it treats those farmed McFish as if they were the equivalent of the wild fish — fungible commodities, in the tongue of economists, like so many aluminum ingots or hundredweight of hard winter wheat. But they are not the same. A pen-raised Atlantic salmon from Chile or Puget Sound is made of different stuff than a wild sockeye or chinook, as significantly different as orange soda and orange juice. As importantly, it is a tendril of an entirely different system of provision and exchange, one which ignores the distinct qualities of local varieties and cultures and instead seeks to produce More of whatever Product can be sold at a profit. In an economy rooted in conservation, those differences between local strains of salmon — and apples and timber — are noted, celebrated, sought after, and accounted for. We see beginnings of that appreciation in the media barrage surrounding the Copper River kings, an early-season run of Alaskan chinook that have captured the attention of gourmet chefs and upscale supermarkets, with attendant high prices to the fishers who net them.

Consideration for the particulars of individual runs can help not just the fishers, but also the fish. One couple whose work demonstrates that possibility is Fred and Linda Hawkshaw, who fish for salmon out of Prince Rupert, B.C. While some of their hot-headed neighbors were blockading the Alaska ferry in 1997, the Hawkshaws were developing a new technique for catching sockeye that relied on snagging the fish by a flap of cartilage on their jaws, rather than trapping them by the gills. Fishing out of Prince Rupert was restricted because coho salmon were scarce that year, and setting nets to catch the more plentiful sockeye would inevitably capture some coho as well. But with the Hawkshaws' method, those coho could be released unharmed. Since the fish were alive when they were removed from the net, another advantage was that the fish could be bled and gutted as soon as they were killed, yielding a higher-quality product than most gill-net boats produce. With marketing help from Ecotrust Canada (a Vancouver-based nonprofit), the Hawkshaws began to ship their fish to high-end Vancouver markets, realizing more than $3 a pound for their fish (compared with under a dollar for their fellow fishers), compensating them for the extra care they put into the process.

Yankee fisherman Fred March took another tack. The 60-year-old

March fished as a young man in Puget Sound, and later off Alaska's Copper River Delta. He now makes his home near the headwaters of the North River, which flows into Washington's Willapa Bay, and gill-nets there as well as in Alaska. But fish runs in Willapa are faltering, in part because of damage to spawning and rearing grounds on the North. So March turned part of his 93-acre homestead into a salmon-rearing complex, with a sinuous network of channels and ponds where young fish can hatch and grow. At first he stocked it with surplus eggs from a state hatchery which he layered in gravel and tended until the fry emerged. After a few years his supply of eggs was cut off, so he dug an extra thousand feet of channel, filled it with gravel and flowing water, opened a fish ladder between his waterways and the river, then watched as adult salmon swam up, mated and laid eggs in the space he'd prepared. In 1996, his best year, this prosthetic habitat was home to 300 thousand eggs of chum, chinook, and coho salmon and steelhead trout. March still fishes at the mouth of the North River, but he lets the fish runs dictate his fishing. In 1995 and 1996, he took about a thousand fish a year, but in 1997 when it became apparent that the coho run was weak, he pulled his nets out of the water to let as many fish make it upriver as possible.

March's operation is much less invasive than a hatchery: fish that use his site do so because they have chosen it. They select their own mates, and the young feed on the aquatic insects that thrive in March's ponds and channels until they decide to swim down the fish ladder to the river below. His approach bears the mark of a properly humble salmon project: it minimizes human interference with what ought to be the fish's own business.

In each location, that principle plays out differently. In Young's Bay near the mouth of the Columbia, technicians raise fingerlings in pens in a watershed where the native fish runs were extinguished long ago. The fry imprint on the bay as their home place, so when they return as adults, they mill around the estuary and provide easy targets for a small gill-net fishing fleet that can seek them without fear of incidentally entangling fish from endangered stocks. This project avoids some of the pitfalls of an upriver hatchery, because the fish it releases don't compete with wild stocks in the river en route to the ocean. They home in on a watershed that lacks wild spawners, so they separate themselves from their wild cousins when they return. It's not like a fish farm, because the fingerlings are raised only for a few months, then turned loose to roam the ocean for two or three years. They feed out there, sparing the bay the impacts it would suffer from the untreated excreta of large penned fish.

At the same time, it limits demand for fish meal that would be produced by a deep-sea trawler fleet scooping up fish indiscriminately, thereby putting ocean food webs at risk.

Because the Young's Bay fishery is selective, some of the fish from it — bled and iced to preserve freshness — have been marketed as environmentally benign: salmon that can be consumed without the fear of accidentally eating the last spawner of a run. This selectivity is a hallmark of fisheries that care as much for posterity as for profit — a quality appreciated by a small but growing number of fishmongers and their customers. "There are a lot of people really interested in being as low-impact as possible when they buy seafood," says Seattle-based fish dealer John Foss. "We market our fish as harvested from intact, healthy runs." Makers of products whose production affects fish — from electricity to wine — cater to this concern, too, with labeling programs called "Salmon Safe" and "Fish Friendly."

Perhaps the ultimate in the precise harvest of salmon is a tribal fishery on the Nass River in British Columbia. Members of the Nisga'a First Nation make use of fishwheels, an elegant and ancient technology. The river current spins the curved paddles on the wheel, which scoop up fish and deposit them alive in pens at either side of the trap. Rarer species, such as steelhead, can be released. And since the Nisga'a operate traps both high and low in the river, biologists can tag fish near the mouth and learn about the population size by the number of tagged fish caught upriver. This sort of precise information allowed Alaska to rebuild its fisheries after they were decimated in the 1950s by overexploitation, and now enables state biologists to manipulate the openings and closings of the fishing season to achieve their top priority: that enough salmon make it to the spawning grounds to perpetuate the runs.

These salmon stories are some of the modern annals of Salmon Nation. They describe recent acts in the drama of people, fish, and terrain that has been unfolding for as long as humans have inhabited this place. It is a rich and deep connection: the fish have fed us and nourished the soil of our homeland for thousands of years. We have celebrated them in story, song, and statuary, and the land has sheltered us both.

Yet there has been a cooling of relations, a period of misunderstanding and distance. We humans have been less than scrupulous in keeping our common home clean and hospitable for the fish that return with their gifts year after year. We took the salmon for granted. We treated them as objects or products instead of as our cohabitants, and now we are recognizing the results.

But the ties that bind us to the salmon are not beyond repair. The stories in this chapter are just a few of the renewed overtures that people are making to the fish that shaped so much of human culture along the rivers that drain into the Pacific.

As citizens all across the region seek this reconciliation with the salmon, three qualities stand out in their efforts. They treat the gifts of this land with respect. They take note of the fine interplay among all the aspects of this region that contribute to those gifts, from the integrity of the watershed to the health of the forest and the conviviality of the city. And they celebrate the unique qualities of this region we have made home, because there is certainly much that warrants celebration.

People committed to their citizenship in Salmon Nation are practicing these principles, in part because the fish show us so plainly the benefits of adhering to them. As a culture, we may be slow learners, somewhat clumsy and unpolished in our studies. But with the salmon's guidance, we can figure out how to reshape our relations with the landscape to which we, no less than the fish, belong.

RESOURCES

For readers who want to delve more deeply into salmon issues, we offer a few suggestions of how to find out more; for readers inspired to act at the seafood counter, on the stream bank, or in civic life, we offer leads that we hope will help you to connect with an endeavor you find worthwhile.

BECOMING MORE INFORMED

Find salmon news on-line at Tidepool.org

Ecotrust's daily news digest, Tidepool (*www.tidepool.org*), provides summaries of and access to newspaper articles about environment, community, and economy along the coast from Anchorage to San Francisco. Key articles about salmon are archived at *www.tidepool.org/salmon.*

Catch salmon data at Inforain.org

A project of Ecotrust, Inforain makes available data about the region on-line at *www.inforain.org.* The analysis of the status of salmon stocks that is the basis for the maps in this book can be found at *www.inforain. org/salmonstrategy.* You can also investigate the status of salmon and steelhead stocks in specific watersheds at *www.inforain.org/interactivemapping /salmonstock.htm.* One caveat: as on the printed maps in this book, small watersheds are lumped together, and large watersheds are broken up for the purposes of data collection and display.

Hear from the public agencies

Current information about the Endangered Species Act status of U.S. salmon can be found through the National Marine Fisheries Service at *www.nwr.noaa.gov/1salmon/salmesa/index.htm.* British Columbia makes available detailed information about salmon stocks through its website, *www. pac.dfo-mpo.gc.ca/ops/fm/Salmon/index.htm.* For a Native American perspective see the Columbia River Inter-Tribal Fisheries Commission (Yakima, Umatilla, Warm Springs, and Nez Perce), on the web at *www.critfc.org.*

Read all about it

The catalog of salmon books is long and rich. We will mention just a few:

 Reaching Home: Pacific Salmon, Pacific People pairs Natalie Fobes' exquisite photographs of the salmon's life cycle with eloquent essays by sculptor and watershed worker Tom Jay and Brad Matson, former editor of *National Fisherman.* Alaska Northwest Books, 1994, 143 pp., $37.95.

 In the finely crafted *Totem Salmon: Life Lessons from Another Species,*

Freeman House tells the story of his and his neighbors' work to restore salmon runs to the Mattole River in northwestern California, and relates it to a broader context ranging from indigenous ritual to contemporary beliefs about property rights. House's essay in Chapter 4 is adapted from this book. Beacon Press, 1999, 224 pp., $25 hardbound, $16 paperback.

First Fish, First People: Salmon Tales of the North Pacific Rim is a collection of essays, stories, and poetry from native people around the North Pacific Rim, describing their relationship with salmon. Besides people of North America, this book includes work by the Ainu of northern Japan, and indigenous people from Kamchatka and Siberia. Elizabeth Woody's essay in Chapter 1 is adapted from one of her contributions to this book. One Reel and the University of Washington Press, 1998, 204 pp., $24.95.

Jim Lichatowich's book *Salmon Without Rivers: A History of the Pacific Salmon Crisis* shows how attempts to manage salmon populations and substitute for the natural qualities of their habitat have failed to stem their decline. Island Press, 1999, 352 pp., $30 hardbound, $18 paperback.

Terry Glavin's book *Dead Reckoning: Confronting the Crisis in Pacific Fisheries* puts salmon issues in a broader context of the destruction of community fisheries, the processing companies' increasing control over boats and fishing licenses, and the widespread impacts on marine life up and down the West Coast. Mountaineers Books, 1997, 181 pp., $15.95.

An artful children's book about salmon is *Swimmer*, by Shelley Gill with illustrations by Shannon Cartwright. It describes the adventures of a salmon's migrations as told to a young Alaskan girl. Paws IV Publishing (Homer, Alaska), 1995, 32 pp., $15.95 hardbound, $8.95 paperback.

For more detail about the salmon's life cycle and suggestions of where and when to observe salmon migrations and spawning, try *Field Guide to the Pacific Salmon*, by Robert Steelquist and the Adopt-A-Stream Foundation. Sasquatch Books, 1992, 64 pp., $7.95 paperback.

Fish on Film

The Return of the Salmon uses historical footage and contemporary interviews to explain the natural history and current state of the salmon in the Pacific Northwest. For more info about this half-hour documentary by Joseph Cone, produced in 1995 by Oregon Sea Grant, check *seagrant. oregonstate.edu/sgpubs/multimedia.html*; the video can be ordered for $20 by calling (800) 375-9360.

Thinking Like A Watershed is Johan Carlisle's half-hour documentary about salmon restoration efforts in the Mattole watershed of northern California. It is available from the Video Project, (800) 475-2638 and described more fully at *www.videoproject.org/ThinkingLikeAWatershed.html*.

FAVORING WILD FISH

Eat the wild ones

Salmon caught in the wild are great food, but unfortunately, only half of the world market in salmon is composed of fish captured from native or hatchery runs. The rest comes from fish farms, with all the related problems described in Chapter 3. Atlantic salmon in the marketplace are all the product of fish farms, as are some chinook and coho.

As a seasonal food, wild salmon used to be unavailable during the colder months of the year. New flash freezing methods offer the option of tasty wild salmon year-round, and high-quality smoked salmon is always available. For recipes and a list of restaurants featuring wild salmon in Seattle, Portland, and the San Francisco Bay area, see *www.salmonnation.com*.

For information about other kinds of seafood and the health of the fisheries that they are derived from, check out the list published by the Monterey Bay Aquarium in California. They've divided seafoods into three categories: best choices, potential problems, and ones to avoid. See the Seafood Watch section of their website, *www.montereybayaquarium.org*. The Audubon Society's Living Oceans campaign offers another good guide and related materials for consumers, at *www.audubon.org/campaign/lo/seafood*.

Farming with fish in mind

Launched in 1995 by the Pacific Rivers Council, Salmon-Safe works to restore water quality and habitat in Pacific Northwest salmon watersheds by evaluating farm operations that use conservation practices benefiting native salmon. Operations endorsed by its independent professional certifiers bear the Salmon-Safe label. More than 30,000 acres have been certified Salmon-Safe in critical Northwest agricultural watersheds. For more information about participating growers and where to find these products, check out their website at *www.salmonsafe.org* or call (503) 232-3750.

WADING RIGHT IN

In the southern parts of Salmon Nation, where damage has been done to fish habitat, there are opportunities to help nature heal that damage. Groups have formed all over the region to undertake this work, and to create a climate in which people act to protect and enhance salmon habitat. For the Sake of the Salmon serves as a networking umbrella for these organizations in California, Oregon, and Washington, and can help you find a group near you from among the more than four hundred they are aware of. For the Sake of the Salmon can be reached at (503) 223-8511 or *www.4sos.org*.

GETTING POLITICAL

Salmon range so widely that they depend on responsible human behavior in arenas from fishing harvest to streamside protection and road building, from the high seas to the highest peaks of their home watersheds. As a heritage we all hold in common, it is only natural that they have become the subject of political decision-making about everything from dam construction and logging rules to the length of fishing seasons.

Arranged around these issues are a host of groups of many stripes. Sometimes it seems that there are as many different styles of political action on behalf of the salmon as there are runs of coho on the West Coast. If you are moved to become involved in some way in support of the salmon and our relations with them, you will find many groups from which to choose. One gateway to finding those organizations is Save Our Wild Salmon, a coalition of dozens of independent groups. You can find out about their campaigns and some of their member organizations through the SOWS website at *www.wildsalmon.org*, or by calling 1-800-SOS-SALMON (1-800-767-7256).

In British Columbia, the David Suzuki Foundation is at the center of many of the political fights being waged over salmon policy. You can contact them at (604) 732-4228 or check their website, *www.davidsuzuki.org*.

ABOUT THIS BOOK

In 1995, Ecotrust published *The Rain Forests of Home: An Atlas of People and Place*, a large-format map atlas designed to raise awareness of the bond between people and forests along the rain forest coast between San Francisco and Anchorage, roughly the territory that some call "Cascadia."

We intended then to create a series of such atlases. We imagined they might become standard references for serious students of the region, each edition a tool for those willing to look beyond arbitrary political boundaries and glimpse the unifying themes of life along this coast.

It was natural that we would turn to salmon, emblematic of the region and at the center of a sustaining economic relationship between people and nature that has endured more than ten thousand years. As salmon hit the front pages with startling population declines, recent Endangered Species Act listings, and U.S.-Canada diplomacy, we realized that few residents had access to the coast-wide "big picture" that could put into context the local salmon story as they lived it.

Salmon Nation is meant to remind all who inhabit or visit the Pacific Northwest that the character, fecundity, and much of the richest history of this place revolve around the abundant presence of these extraordinary fish.

At Ecotrust, we promote an economy built of relationships that restore such abundance and diversity to our lands and waters. We believe that the marketplace can become one of several arenas where community desires are reconciled with the needs of the salmon and our need to connect with them.

We hope this book helps you to live more knowledgeably and deliberately as a citizen of Salmon Nation, and we invite your comments and reactions.

Salmon Nation emerged like a fingerling from the gravels of a coast-wide study of Pacific salmon distribution and abundance begun in 1995 under the direction of Peter Schoonmaker, Ph.D., using computer-based geographic information systems (GIS) technology and a mapping methodology developed by Edward Backus. The team involved in that analysis between 1996 and 1998 included Jon Bowers, Ted Gresh, Erin Kellogg, Jim Lichatowich, Richard Manning, Hans D. Radtke, Dorie Roth, and Cleve Steward.

Individuals responsible for GIS mapping for that study and the creation of original maps for this book include David Albert, David Carruthers, Dorie Roth, and Debra Sohm. We are grateful to Oregon Trout, Kim Hyatt (Department of Fisheries and Oceans), and Alex Wertheimer (Alaska Department of Fish and Game) for sharing data sets we have used in the compilation of these maps and for participating in the analysis. Biologist Willa Nehlsen graciously shared her knowledge, data, and contacts throughout this project, and more than one hundred other fisheries scientists helped to fill our information gaps.

Our colleagues Spencer Beebe, Jennifer Froistad, Ian Gill, and Ed Hunt offered valuable advice and encouragement during the development of the book; Elizabeth Grossman proofread the essays; Ellen Chu (Northwest Environment Watch) shared valuable lessons from her experience of taking manuscripts into print; and John Javna sharpened our thinking about what makes a book appealing.

We owe a special debt to *Chinook Observer* publisher Matt Winters, who shared his personal collection of historic salmon can labels, on which the book's design is based. We are grateful to the Columbia River Maritime Museum for access to their collections of salmon can labels, to Katie Doka for her beautiful cover art and the salmon steak illustration in Chapter 3, to Steve Blackburn for the boat illustrations in Chapter 4, to Shari Erickson and Joe Tomelleri for the salmon illustrations that accompany the map portfolio, and to photographers Gary Braasch and Adrian Dorst for the use of their images. Alex Blendl supplied an historic photograph, and the Oregon Historical Society provided access and permission to reproduce images from its collections.

Bryan and Eldon Potter of Bryan Potter Design in Portland immediately understood our vision for the book and adeptly translated our notions into a graphic treatment. Laura Anderson and her colleagues at the Hatfield Marine Science Center in Newport, Oregon, and Jim Bergeron of the Oregon Sea Grant program in Astoria, offered helpful comments on the illustration of West Coast fishing boats in Chapter 4.

This book and the research and computer mapping that underlie it were made possible by the generosity of Ecotrust's donors and supporters, particularly by project grants from the Compton Foundation, the Giles W. and Elise G. Mead Foundation, the M. J. Murdock Charitable Trust, the Prospect Hill Foundation, and communications support from The Ford Foundation. General support from the Bullitt Foundation, the William and Flora Hewlett Foundation, and the Moore Family Foundation has been invaluable during the course of our work on this book.

We thank our colleagues at Ecotrust and Ecotrust Canada, who have provided support, encouragement, and friendship through many twists and turns along the path to *Salmon Nation*. Finally, we would like to acknowledge and thank the community-builders, conservation entrepreneurs, and Native and non-native fishing families, too numerous to name individually, who believe against all odds that salmon will one day thread the waterways of Salmon Nation in their accustomed abundance and reconstitute our common wealth.

The value in this book is due to all who have shared so generously of their time, resources, and knowledge in its creation. We alone take responsibility for any errors that remain.

For assistance with the updated edition, the editors wish to thank Sam Beebe, Eileen Brady, Analisa Gunnell, Andrea Hildebrand, DeL'Aurore Kyly, Kara Orvieto, Debra Sohm, and Melissa Tatge of Ecotrust. We are grateful to the Gordon and Betty Moore Foundation, the Jyn Foundation, and to Patagonia for support that will help Ecotrust to distribute the book. Our special thanks to communications manager Howard Silverman, who kept this fish swimming in the right direction.

— E.C.W. and S.Z., Portland, March 2003

CONTRIBUTORS

Freeman House, a former commercial salmon fisherman, is co-founder of the Mattole Salmon Group and of the Mattole Restoration Council. He lives in Petrolia, in northwestern California. *Totem Salmon* (Beacon, 1999), from which his essay was excerpted, is his first book.

Jim Lichatowich is an independent biologist who has spent more than thirty years in salmon management and research. Co-author of the landmark 1991 *Fisheries* paper "Pacific salmon at the crossroads," he is the author of *Salmon Without Rivers* (Island Press, 1999). He lives in Columbia City, Oregon.

Richard Manning's six books include *Inside Passage* (Island Press, 2001) and *Food's Frontier* (North Point, 2000). His forthcoming book *Against the Grain* (North Point) argues that 10,000 years of agriculture have damaged both nature and human nature. He has worked as a newspaper editor and reporter in the northern Rockies, and now lives in Montana.

Dorie Roth holds a masters degree in geography from Portland State University and works as a Geographic Information Systems (GIS) analyst at Ecotrust, in Portland, Oregon. A former Class V river guide, she is currently at work on a project to map the status of salmon stocks throughout their natural range on both sides of the North Pacific.

Edward Wolf's work for conservation organizations has taken him from the headwaters of the Amazon to the mouth of the Yukon River. Formerly the communications director at Ecotrust in Portland, Oregon, he is the author of *A Tidewater Place* (Mountaineers Books, 1993) and co-editor of *The Rain Forests of Home* (Island Press, 1997).

Elizabeth Woody (Navajo/Warm Springs/Wasco/Yakama) writes poetry, short fiction, essays, and is a visual artist. Her poetry collection *Hand Into Stone* (The Eighth Mountain Press, 1994) received the American Book Award. She works at Ecotrust, and is enrolled in the Hatfield School of Government at Portland State University.

Seth Zuckerman's writing has appeared in *The Christian Science Monitor*, *Sierra*, and numerous other publications. As chief correspondent for Ecotrust's on-line news service Tidepool.org, he covers the relations between people and the rest of the natural world along the coast from Anchorage to San Francisco. His home is on California's Mattole River.